Endorsements

"Thank you to Gabe Rodriguez for being inspired to write *The Christmas Story: The Father*. He has created an impactful yet simple and incredibly fun book. This literary treasure paves the way to create a valuable tradition that my family will enjoy every year during the Christmas season. I love how Gabe delivers many of the best stories of the Bible — from creation to the birth of our Lord and Savior — in a concise manner. The "Why This Story Matters" section at the end of each day ties the perfect bow on the stories. It all comes together with storytelling, life application, prayer, and references to provide a complete masterpiece for the ages. Well done!"

Chris Larson
FCA Sports Director
Fellowship of Christian Athletes

"Having used a variety of family Advent devotionals when my children were younger, I wish I had *The Christmas Story: The Father* then. It takes the traditional Advent devotional to the next level by exposing us to the true beginning of the Father's working of his gift to the world (Jesus, his Son) through the Old Testament. The book also serves as a good introduction to the Old Testament with easy-to-understand applications of themes and the importance of scriptural stories. I look forward to using this devotional with my grandchildren one day."

Todd Crippin
President
JMH Publishing
Keep Start Stop Deliver: An Active Devotional
Keep Start Stop Deliver: A Prayer Companion

"Gabe Rodriguez is a good friend, and I have been fortunate to have a front row seat to the work God has been doing in his life over the past five years. He has a heart and a mission to connect every person, especially young people, to the word of God and the life-changing power of the Gospel of Jesus Christ. *The Christmas Story: The Father* accomplishes that mission by simply and clearly connecting the stories of the Old Testament to humanity's need for a savior and the fulfillment of that need in the person of Christ. A great Advent devotional and new tradition that will prepare you and your family for the Christmas season."

Nate Lien
Founder and Partner
KCN Companies

"This biblically based book is a perfect addition to your Advent journey, allowing you the opportunity to dive into the living Word in bite-sized pieces. The easy-to-follow layout gives families a profound way to stay grounded in the true meaning of Christmas. Each day, you will be guided through stories in the Bible, coupled with reflection and heartfelt prayer. *The Christmas Story: The Father* is a perfect gift for your family legacy and for all families seeking to know and understand the true love and mercy of God."

"Ask and it will be given to you; seek and you will find; knock and the door will be opened to you. For everyone who asks receives; the one who seeks finds; and to the one who knocks, the door will be opened" (Mathew 7:7–8).

Cindy Mencacci
Former Sales Executive
Wife, mother, grandmother, and follower of Jesus Christ

THE CHRISTMAS STORY

The Father

Gabe Rodriguez

The Christmas Story
The Father
Gabe Rodriguez

3 in 1 Press, Shawnee, Kansas

Editor: Kim Fletcher

Cover and Interior design: DavisCreativePublishing.com

Publisher's Cataloging-in-Publication
Names: Rodriguez, Gabe, author.
Title: The Christmas story. The Father / Gabe Rodriguez.
Other titles: Father
Description: Shawnee, Kansas : 3 in 1 Press, [2025] | Includes bibliographical references.
Identifiers: ISBN: 9798993520209 (paperback) | 9798993520216 (ebook) | 9798993520223 (hardback)
Subjects: LCSH: Jesus Christ--Nativity--Biblical teaching. | Virgin birth--Biblical teaching. | Christmas. | God--Love. | Devotional calendars. | LCGFT: Devotional literature. | BISAC: RELIGION / Holidays / Christmas & Advent. | RELIGION / Christian Living / Devotional. | RELIGION / Christian Education / General.
Classification: LCC: BT315.3 .R64 2025 | DDC: 232.92--dc23

ATTENTION CORPORATIONS, UNIVERSITIES, COLLEGES, NOT-FOR-PROFITS, AND PROFESSIONAL ORGANIZATIONS: Quantity discounts are available on bulk purchases of this book for educational, gift purposes, or as premiums for increasing magazine subscriptions or renewals. Special books or book excerpts can also be created to fit specific needs. For information, please contact Gabe Rodriguez, 3 in 1 Press, 3in1press@gmail.com, and www.3in1press.com

DEDICATION

To Benjamin and Samuel,
my inspiration for writing this book.
Being your dad is the
greatest blessing of my life.

Table of Contents

Foreword

You hold in your hands the fruit of a dad's deep desire to share the timeless truth and meaning of Christmas with his two sons. After a frustrating and unsuccessful attempt, he nearly gave up. But the Holy Spirit refused to let that spark fade. Instead, He kindled it into a burning hunger for God's Word — a yearning to uncover the foundational truths of the Christmas story and present them in a way that was simple, accessible, and compelling for all: young or old, seasoned or new to faith.

Day after day, night after night, Gabe found himself drawn to Scripture and then to his keyboard. This God-given mission consumed his thoughts — an unrelenting drive to share the Word.

It wasn't until the manuscript was nearly complete that Gabe reached out to me. We met briefly at a men's Bible study that my son invited me to. In May 2025, I received a text from Gabe asking to meet and discuss the book he was working on. He wanted feedback — and a pastor's perspective.

I vividly remember our conversation at a neighborhood coffee shop. Gabe's passion was unmistakable, pouring out of him and onto the pages of his book. He asked for my thoughts on the concept, the Trinitarian structure of three volumes, and the format of the daily readings. I offered some initial feedback, and a few weeks later, my son handed me a three-ring binder containing Gabe's rough draft.

It didn't take long to see the clarity and intentionality of the layout: explanatory subtitles, distilled stories, and powerful truths — each leading to another story, another truth, and ultimately, to salvation in Christ. But the true gem of each page was the section titled *Why This Story Matters*. This is the heart of Gabe's work: helping readers apply eternal truths to their lives in practical, relatable, and contemporary ways.

As a parish pastor for over forty years, I've witnessed one of the greatest challenges in the church: the struggle of parents to pass on their faith to their children and grandchildren. Gabe confronts this challenge head-on, weaving into his book a meaningful solution. In the back pages, you'll find space to record names, dates, and moments when these stories are shared, literally documenting the passing of the torch from one generation to the next.

Shortly after reading Gabe's manuscript, I visited our daughter's home. She and her husband are raising four of our nine grandchildren. On the kitchen wall, I saw a quote from John Piper that struck me deeply:

"I have told you before that your mother and I will probably not be able to pass on to you any kind of earthly inheritance. If we can pass on to you a passion for God, however, we will have given you something more valuable than silver, gold, or rubies and more satisfying than anything a mortal can experience." —From *Don't Waste Your Life* (Proverbs 3:13–15)

Read this book. Share these stories. For as the Apostle Paul reminds us:

"No eye has seen, no ear has heard, and no mind has imagined what God has prepared for those who love him" (1 Corinthians 2:9, NLT).

The Reverend Dr. Stephen C. Lien
Kansas City, Missouri

Preface

For most of my life, I was a lukewarm Christian. I believed in God and that His Son, Jesus, was sent, died, and rose again for the forgiveness of our sins. But that was about where my faith began and ended.

I went to church once or twice a month, always on the big days like Christmas Eve and Easter. My prayer life was inconsistent, and I rarely opened my Bible. Honestly, I didn't know where to start, and the Bible felt overwhelming to try to tackle on my own.

Over the years, my wife and I joined different Bible studies. I attended various groups for almost a decade, but I treated them more as social gatherings than opportunities to grow closer to God. Most weeks, I came unprepared, cramming for the lesson just before it began.

This pattern continued for about twenty years. I stayed spiritually stuck in neutral, doing the bare minimum but expecting my life to somehow feel different and full of God's purpose. Deep down, I knew something was missing.

About five years ago, I reached a breaking point. I grew tired of relying on my pastor, my friends, or the faith of others to miraculously "rub off" on me. I realized and accepted the awful truth: My faith wasn't growing because I wasn't putting in the effort. And worse, I failed to lead my family spiritually. I had a wonderful wife and two boys, but I relied on my wife, the boys' school, and our church to teach my sons the most important lesson in life — what it looks like to be a Christian man — instead of taking responsibility myself.

So, I made up my mind: I was going all in.

I began to serve and attend church more regularly. I came to Bible study prepared and started reading Scripture on my own consistently. I explored resources like The Bible Project and was challenged to complete a one-year Bible reading plan by Tara-Leigh Cobble. I also began reading works by N. T. Wright, which deepened my understanding of the gospel.

What began as a discipline turned into a joy. After a couple of years, my Bible study leader asked me to co-lead our men's group. I felt my life changing. My heart transformed as I focused less on *my* plans and more on *God's* plans for my life.

But even as I grew, I struggled to pass that growth on to my family. I wanted to help my boys understand the true meaning of Christmas and why Jesus came, but I wasn't sure how to make that connection. Every December, it felt like the holiday was buried under shopping lists, travel plans, and endless to-do lists. The true meaning of Christmas was getting lost.

One year, I tried reading a chapter of the book of Luke with my boys each day from December 1 through December 24. It was my attempt to make the true meaning of Christmas a priority in our home. The idea sounded great, but it quickly fell apart. After a few days, they were clearly disengaged. They didn't understand the language, and while Luke beautifully tells the story of Jesus' life, it didn't explain why His birth was necessary in a way they could grasp.

Over the next couple of years, I searched everywhere for a resource that would connect with kids, teens, or even new believers. I wanted a way to explain the story of Jesus' birth in the larger context of God's plan … why the world needed a Savior and why His arrival changed everything. I tried bookstores, websites, and looked through many devotionals, but I couldn't find what I was looking for.

So, in 2024, prompted by the Holy Spirit, I was led to write it.

This book brings together the most important stories, from Creation to the birth of Jesus, showcasing God's love for us, humanity's repeated failures, and our desperate need for redemption. It explains why Jesus came as the perfect, blameless sacrifice for our sins. Because we could never reconcile ourselves to God on our own.

My hope is simple: that families like mine will read these stories each December and refocus their hearts on what Christmas truly means. I want my boys to grow up believing in the God who loves them and understanding why Jesus' birth is the greatest gift ever given. And one day, I pray they will carry this tradition on to their own families, passing down the true story of Christmas for generations to come.

How To Use This Book

Overview

First and foremost, this book is not meant to replace the Bible, the living Word of God. The Bible holds immeasurable value. Its pages are filled with life lessons, truth, and history that serve as our moral compass, showing us how to live the lives God intends for us.

The Christmas Story: The Father is designed as an introduction to the Old Testament (the first 39 books of the Bible). It presents key stories in a clear, chronological, and easily digestible format, connecting one story to the next so readers can better understand how some of the most well-known biblical events fit together as part of God's larger plan.

The purpose of this book is to help reveal the "why" behind the coming of Jesus — why He was sent on our behalf — and to help us remember the true meaning of Christmas. Humanity, in all its brokenness, could never save or reconcile itself to the Father. So, God sent His Son, Jesus Christ, a perfect and blameless sacrifice, to become the Savior of the world.

My hope is that everyone who reads this book will:

1. Understand who God is.
2. See how loving God is.
3. Remember why Jesus was sent.
4. Realize that God sees each of us and that we all matter.
5. Understand that each of us was created with a purpose.
6. Use this book as a guide to the Old Testament.
7. See the Bible not as an ancient book of the past, but as a living guide for today.
8. Create meaningful Christian family traditions.

When Should I Read This Book?

Every Christmas Season:

This book is designed to be read from December 1 through December 27 every year. It invites individuals and families to slow down, reflect, and return to the true meaning of Christmas and create a meaningful tradition that keeps Christ at the center of the season.

Any Time of Year:

Although written with the Advent season in mind, you can also read this book at any time of the year to gain a deeper understanding of the Old Testament.

For Bible Study:

The Christmas Story: The Father can also serve as a 27-day Bible study. Read one story each day, then gather to discuss what stood out to you. Reflect on the "Why This Story Matters" section. Ask yourself: How does this apply to my life or my family? What part of the story speaks to my heart? Use these reflections to grow together in faith with family and friends alike.

What is the Purpose of the Family Scroll?

Many of us have family traditions passed down through generations — recipes shared, heirlooms treasured, or stories retold. These keepsakes remind us of where we come from and the people who came before us. But how do we pass on our *faith* to the next generation?

As a parent, I've worked hard to teach my boys courtesy and good manners: open the door for others, say "please" and "thank you," offer a firm handshake, keep your elbows off the table. Yet, I've often wondered, how do I ensure they also inherit my *faith*? How will they one day pass *that* on to their own families?

Those questions inspired what I call **The Family Scroll** at the end of this book. It's a space for you and your family to record your belief in the Trinity series I've been led to write — the Father, the Son, and the Holy Spirit. Like a family tree, it allows you to document who you believe in, where you came from, what your purpose is, and why Jesus was sent for you.

My hope is that as you read *The Christmas Story: The Father*, you'll record the year you first read and believed each story, then continue marking each time you revisit them, whether that's annually or multiple times during the year. Over time, your Family Scroll will tell a beautiful story of faith handed down generation after generation so that one day your children, grandchildren, and great-grandchildren will see their names among those who believed before them.

Imagine being a young boy or girl reading *The Christmas Story: The Father* for the first time, and at the end of the book, signing your name beneath those of your family members who have read and believed these same stories for decades — or even centuries. That's powerful. That's legacy. That's faith passed on.

What Do the Colors on the Cover Mean?

Blue (The Father):

Blue is the color of Advent, the season of hope, peace, joy, and love leading up to Christmas. It symbolizes the hope we have in the Father, whose promise was fulfilled through the birth of His Son, Jesus Christ.

Green (The Son):

The color green symbolizes new life and renewal, seen each spring as the earth comes alive after winter. For believers, it represents spiritual growth, revival, and a faith that continues to mature throughout life. Through our belief in Jesus Christ, we are made new and grow daily in His grace.

Red (The Holy Spirit):

Red symbolizes both power and sacrifice. It represents the fire of the Holy Spirit that came down at Pentecost and the courage it gave the apostles to spread the Gospel. Red also reminds us of the blood of Jesus poured out for our sins and the sacrifice of those who carried, and continue to carry, His message to the ends of the earth.

Why Are There Dates at the Beginning of Each Story?

Dates found throughout this book are approximate. Biblical scholars and historians often differ on the exact years of events in Scripture. I don't claim to be a historian, and the dates provided aren't meant to be exact, but they are directionally accurate and organized in chronological order to help readers follow the timeline of God's unfolding story. You'll see the symbol (~) before each date, acknowledging that while specific years may vary slightly depending on the source, the heart and message of each story remain unchanged.

Introduction: The Father

In the beginning, God spoke a perfect world into existence and filled it with life, beauty, and love. He made the sea, the land, the sky, and the moon. He named every animal and gave every living creature a purpose. And finally, God made mankind. Adam and Eve, man and woman, in His own image. He breathed them into life, placed them in the Garden of Eden, walked with them, and gave them everything they needed to make a good life and home. In the Garden, there was no pain, no fear, no fighting, shame, or worry. Only peace, trust, happiness, and love.

But then temptation entered the Garden, and that time of peace changed forever.

Adam and Eve heard a lie, believed it, and made a choice. They disobeyed God's command not to eat from the Tree of Life, and in an instant, they lost something precious. The special relationship that God established between Himself and His people was broken. Sin entered the world and spread from generation to generation, like an illness running rampant. Pain, sadness, and separation overcame the beauty God created.

Still, God never gave up on us.

God used Noah, Abraham, Moses, Joseph, and David to share messages of truth and call His people back to Himself. God made promises to His people, performed miracles, gave His people laws, and sent prophets with warnings. But stubbornness prevailed, and humanity continued to do wicked things.

They'd cry out for help, and God showed them mercy again and again. This pattern repeated itself for many years: faithfulness, followed by rebellion; worship followed by idolatry; obedience followed by selfish pride. When God's people cried out in need, He answered with grace. Yet, eventually, they turned away from Him once more.

It was obvious: Mankind could not save itself.

Even religion, which was meant to bring people closer to God, became twisted. What started out as building a relationship turned into a checklist. People offered sacrifices and prayers without sincerity or passion. They loved to honor God with their lips, but their hearts and actions were far from Him. Society ignored the downtrodden, and those in authority ruled without mercy. Greed, lust, pride, and violence filled people's hearts and minds. Instead of loving one's neighbor, they only looked out for themselves, chasing after wealth, status, and power.

Yet God had a plan to address humanity's brokenness.

He promised a Savior — One who would take away the sins of the world. A humble King who would serve rather than be served. This Messiah — the "anointed One" — would transform our broken hearts from the inside out.

And so, in the middle of the night, heaven touched earth. God sent His only Son — Jesus — not to a fancy palace, but to a lonely stable. Not to live among royalty, but born to a young woman and a carpenter of modest means. Jesus came into the world wrapped in humility, God Himself, entering our brokenness not in power, but in love, so that we might one day be made whole again.

~ 4000 Years Before Christ (BC)

God Creates the World

In the Beginning

In the beginning, before time started, before heaven or earth were created, before there was light or darkness, before people or animals existed, there was nothing … nothing except God, our Father and Creator. There was only endless space, waiting to be filled by His imagination and His love.

Then, God spoke the world into existence.

Day One: Day and Night

"Let there be light," He said, and there was light. God separated the light from the darkness. He called the light "day," and the darkness He called "night." There was evening, and there was morning, the first day (Genesis 1:1–5).

Day Two: The Heavens Above

The next day, God said, "Let there be a great space above the waters." And He called the space "sky." It stretched farther than the eye could see, filled with air to breathe and clouds to bring rain. That was the second day (Genesis 1:6–8).

Day Three: Land, Sea, and Plants

Then God said, "Let the waters below the sky come together so that dry land can appear." He called the dry ground "land," and the gathered waters, "seas." He covered the land with hills, mountains, rivers, and valleys. Then He filled it with plants, trees, vegetables, fruits, and flowers, each one able to grow and produce more of its kind. That was the third day (Genesis 1:9–13).

Day Four: The Lights Above

Next, God created two great lights. He made the sun to shine during the day and the moon to light the night. He also placed stars in the sky to twinkle and sparkle. These lights would help people know when to plant, when to harvest, and how to keep track of time. That was the fourth day (Genesis 1:14–19).

Day Five: Creatures in the Sea and the Air

Then God filled the seas with life. Fish of every size and color swam through the water. He also made birds to soar through the sky and sing heavenly songs. And God blessed each of its kind, saying, "Be fruitful and increase in number and fill the water in the seas, and let the birds increase on the earth" (Genesis 1:22). That was the fifth day (Genesis 1:20–23).

Day Six: Animals of Every Kind and People

Then God said, "Let the land be filled with living creatures." And it was. He made every kind of animal — giraffes and goats, lions and lemurs, bobcats and buffalo. He made them all unique and for a special purpose. That was the sixth day (Genesis 1:24–25).

But God wasn't finished.

In His Image: God Created Mankind

God did something extraordinary: He made people in His own image. First, He formed Adam, a man, and later, Eve, a woman. God gave them the ability to love, to choose, to create, and to care. He blessed them and gave them a beautiful place to live called the Garden of Eden. He told them, "You are free to eat from any tree in the garden, except for one, the Tree of the Knowledge of Good and Evil. If you eat from it, you will surely die" (Genesis 1:26–31; 2:7–9, 15–17, 21–22).

God gave them authority over the fish in the sea, the birds in the sky, and all the animals that walk the earth (Genesis 1:28). He looked at everything He had made, and it was very good (Genesis 1:31).

Day Seven: A Holy Day of Rest

On the seventh day, God rested, not because He was tired, but because His creation was complete. He blessed the seventh day and made it holy (Genesis 2:1–3).

The world had begun, spoken into motion by the breath of God, full of life, adventure, hope, and love.

Why This Story Matters

The creation story reminds us just how powerful, intentional, and loving God is. He didn't just create a world that functions, He created one that is full of beauty and wonder. He filled it with light and darkness, sun and stars, oceans, mountains, seasons, animals, and every kind of plant and food we would need. On top of that, He gave it all to us as a gift, asking nothing in return but our love and trust.

God didn't create people like robots who were forced to obey Him. Instead, He gave us something incredible — the freedom to choose. We can choose to love Him, to trust Him, and to follow Him with our whole hearts. That freedom is part of what it means to be made in His image, reflecting His heart and character in how we live and love.

From the very beginning, God had a plan. Nothing was random or accidental. He created everything with purpose, including us, and He called it all "good."

A Prayer to End

Dear God, thank You for creating this beautiful world. Thank You for making the sun and the sky, the land and the seas, and all the animals that live in them. Thank You for making us in Your image, and for creating each of us with unique gifts and differences. Help us to see the beauty found within all that You've made, and help us care for the world that You have entrusted to us. Amen.

Bible References

Genesis 1:1–5 — Creation of light
Genesis 1:6–8 — Creation of the sky
Genesis 1:9–13 — Land and plants
Genesis 1:14–19 — Sun, moon, and stars
Genesis 1:20–23 — Sea creatures and birds
Genesis 1:24–25 — Land animals
Genesis 1:26–31 — Creation of mankind
Genesis 2:1–3 — God rests
Genesis 2:7–9, 15–17, 21–22 — Adam and Eve, command in the Garden

~ 4000 Years Before Christ (BC)

The Fall of Man — Sin Enters the World

The Garden of Eden

Yes, there was a time when all of creation lived in harmony: after God spoke the world into existence and commanded Adam and Eve not to eat from the Tree of the Knowledge of Good and Evil. God gave Adam and Eve a beautiful home in the Garden of Eden. During that time, they grew close as husband and wife.

Every day, God visited them in the garden. They walked with Him, talked with Him, and explored all the beauty Eden had to offer. When God was near, Adam and Eve listened, learned, and grew in wisdom. They asked questions, discovered their purpose, and, most of all, they simply enjoyed being with Him. It was peaceful, joyful, and full of love.

The Deceptive Serpent

One day, while Eve walked through the garden, a snake, used by Satan, approached her and asked, "Did God really say you must not eat from any tree in the garden?" (Genesis 3:1).

Eve answered, "Yes, He said we must not eat from the Tree of the Knowledge of Good and Evil, or even touch it, or we will die."

The snake replied, "You will not surely die. God just doesn't want you to be like Him, knowing good and evil" (Genesis 3:4–5).

The snake tricked Eve into doubting what God had said. She looked at the fruit. It seemed good to eat. She wanted to be wise. So she reached out, picked it from the tree, and took a bite. Later, she gave some to Adam, and he ate it too (Genesis 3:6).

The Event That Changed Everything

In that moment, everything changed.

Before they ate the fruit, Adam and Eve had never known fear, shame, or doubt. But after eating it, they realized they were naked, and for the first time, they felt embarrassed. They gathered leaves and made coverings for themselves. Then they heard God walking in the Garden.

"Adam, Eve … where are you?" God called (Genesis 3:9).

Instead of running toward God like they used to, they hid behind a tree. Sin had entered the world, and they were afraid. God already knew what had happened, but He still asked, "Why are you hiding? Who told you that you were naked?" In a panic, Adam blamed Eve. Eve blamed the snake. Neither of them took responsibility for what they had done (Genesis 3:10–13).

Consequences of Sin

God was heartbroken. He had given them everything, and now, because of their disobedience, they could no longer stay in Eden. Life outside the Garden would be harder, growing food would take effort, pain and sickness would exist, and their closeness with God would feel far away (Genesis 3:16–19, 23–24).

God Still Loved Them

Despite their actions, God made clothes for them from animal skins before they left the Garden. He still cared for them (Genesis 3:21). And even more amazing, God made them a promise. He said that one day, a Savior would be born from Eve's family line. That Savior would defeat Satan and bring people back into a right relationship with God (Genesis 3:15).

Even though the world was now broken, God's love never ended. His redemption story had only just begun.

Why This Story Matters

This is a story we can all relate to. Like Adam and Eve, we sometimes choose our own way instead of trusting God. We do things we know we shouldn't, and afterward, we might feel ashamed, embarrassed, or guilty. But God doesn't give up on us.

Every moment of temptation is also an opportunity to turn to Him for help to get us through whatever life throws our way. And even when we fail, He still loves us.

This story reminds us that even in our brokenness, God always works to bring us back to Him. From the very beginning, He planned to send Jesus, a Savior who would rescue us and make things right.

A Prayer to End

Dear God, thank You for showing us what unconditional love looks like. Even though Adam and Eve disobeyed, You loved them anyway. Thank You for being a God of second chances. Help us stay out of situations that might tempt us to do something that hurts You. And if we do mess up, help us turn to You, ask for help, and do what's right, even if it's not easy. Thank You for never giving up on us. Amen.

Bible References

Genesis 3:1–5 — The serpent tempts Eve

Genesis 3:6 — Adam and Eve eat the fruit

Genesis 3:8–13 — God confronts Adam and Eve

Genesis 3:14–19 — The consequences of sin

Genesis 3:15 — The first promise of a Savior

Genesis 3:21 — God clothes Adam and Eve

Genesis 3:23–24 — Adam and Eve are sent out of Eden

~ 3900 Years Before Christ (BC)

Cain and Abel — A Selfish Heart

A Different Life

After Adam and Eve were banned from the Garden of Eden, life became much harder (Genesis 3:23–24). They had to work the land just to grow food. Their bodies felt pain, they got sick, and their hearts carried the heaviness of regret. They remembered how easy and peaceful things had been in Eden, when God was always near. Now, outside the Garden, they felt the sadness of being far from Him. Still, even though life was harder, God did not abandon them. He still loved them and stayed true to His plan that would unfold in time.

Two Sons with Different Focus

In the years that followed, Adam and Eve had two sons (Genesis 4:1–2). They named their first Cain, and their second Abel.

Cain and Abel grew up with a love for the outdoors. As they became men, Cain worked the fields as a farmer, and Abel became a shepherd. One day, both brothers decided to bring an offering to God to show their love and trust in Him (Genesis 4:3–4). This was a big deal; food was harder to come by after Adam and Eve sinned in the Garden, so giving part of it to God meant they were showing faith. They were saying, "God, I trust You to provide more. I don't need to keep everything for myself."

Cain brought some of the crops he had grown. Abel brought the best parts of his flock, the finest animals he had.

God Looks Within

God saw their offerings and knew the hearts behind them (Genesis 4:4–5). He was pleased with Abel's gift because Abel gave the best he had, with a heart full of love and trust. But God saw something different with Cain. Cain held back the best for himself. His offering didn't come from a heart of faith. It came from a place of selfishness. That saddened God.

A Warning and a Bad Choice

When Cain noticed that God wasn't pleased with his gift, he got angry and upset. God saw what was happening in Cain's heart and gently asked him:

"Why are you angry? If you do what is right, won't you be accepted? But if you don't, sin is crouching at your door. It wants to rule over you, but you must rule over it." (Genesis 4:6–7)

God gave Cain a chance to make things right, to listen, learn, and try again. But Cain didn't want to hear it. He was so angry he couldn't think straight. He asked Abel to come with him out to a field, and while they were alone, Cain attacked and killed his brother (Genesis 4:8).

The First Life Taken

It was the first time anyone had ever taken another person's life. The sin that started with Adam and Eve had now spread, and it was growing.

Later, God asked Cain, "Where is your brother Abel?" And Cain answered, "I don't know. Am I my brother's keeper?" (Genesis 4:9).

The fact was, Abel was gone, and Cain would carry the weight of that sin for the rest of his life.

Mercy and Judgment

God sent Cain away from his home to live in a land called Nod (Genesis 4:10–12, 16). But even then, God showed mercy. He placed a mark on Cain to protect him so no one would harm him (Genesis 4:15). Though God was deeply hurt by Cain's actions, He still cared for him. And even in this, God's plan moved forward, Cain would go on to have children and start a new part of the human story (Genesis 4:17).

Why This Story Matters

Cain had the opportunity to confess his sins, but his anger clouded his heart and mind. Instead of humbling himself before God, he refused to take responsibility for his actions.

When we make mistakes and bring our shortcomings to God, we are given an opportunity that shapes our character and helps us grow spiritually by drawing us into a closer relationship with Him.

What matters most to God is the condition of our hearts. We cannot fake a generous heart. He sees and knows us completely, understanding when we are selfish with our time and possessions, or when our words do not bring Him glory.

When we freely give of our time, efforts, and resources, like Abel, we demonstrate that we trust God with every part of our lives. Whether it's how we perform in the classroom, at our jobs, or on the sports field, this story reminds us to give God our very best in all we do.

A Prayer to End

Dear God, help us not to be selfish with our things or how we spend our time. Teach us to give You the very best we have, always. Shape our hearts to be kind, generous, and full of Your love, even when we don't agree with others. When we feel angry, jealous, or upset, help us slow down and hear Your calming voice, so we don't make a bad situation worse. Amen.

Biblical References

Genesis 3:23–24 — Adam and Eve are sent out of Eden
Genesis 4:1–2 — Cain and Abel are born
Genesis 4:3–5 — Cain and Abel bring offerings to God
Genesis 4:6–7 — God speaks to Cain about his anger
Genesis 4:8 — Cain kills Abel in the field
Genesis 4:9 — God asks Cain where Abel is
Genesis 4:10–12 — God tells Cain his punishment
Genesis 4:15 — God places a mark on Cain for protection
Genesis 4:16–17 — Cain leaves and begins a new life

~ 2500 Years Before Christ (BC)

Noah and the Ark

After the tragedy between their sons Cain and Abel, Adam and Eve eventually had another child, Seth. Many generations later, Noah was born through Seth's family line. Noah was a man whom God used in a very special way.

During his lifetime, sin and selfishness continued to grow in the hearts of people all over the world. Most had stopped listening to God altogether. Instead, they followed their own ways, doing whatever they wanted without caring about right or wrong. Their hearts were filled with violence, pride, and evil (Genesis 6:5–6).

God looked at everything He had made. What was once beautiful and good had become broken and filled with sorrow. But even in a world filled with darkness, there was one man, Noah, who still walked with God. He was faithful (Genesis 6:8–9).

God's Secret Direction

Noah was a man of great character and kindness. Even though everyone around him focused on doing whatever made them happy, Noah lived by the word of God and did what was right and just (Genesis 6:9).

One day, God spoke to him and gave him an unthinkable task: "Build a great ark, a giant boat, because I am going to send a flood to wash the earth clean. But you and your family will be safe. Bring two of every animal, male and female, into the ark with you" (Genesis 6:13–20).

Noah heard and believed what God told him to do, even though the project in front of him seemed overwhelming. But Noah didn't flinch. He trusted God 100 percent (Genesis 6:22).

Noah Listens and Obeys; Animals Come

Noah followed the exact instructions God gave him and began building the ark, a boat over one football field long and as tall as a four-story building (Genesis 6:15). It had three decks, separate spaces for all the animals, and enough room to store food for every creature and Noah's family.

When Noah finally finished the ark, God performed a miracle. From every corner of the earth, animals began to arrive, male and female, two by two, just as God had said (Genesis 7:8–9).

Horses galloped, lions roared, rabbits hopped, and birds flew through the air and landed gently on the deck of the ark. Each one moved into its space, ready for the journey ahead.

Then Noah and his family — his wife, his sons Shem, Ham, and Japheth, and their wives — entered the ark. And God Himself shut the door (Genesis 7:13–16).

The Great Flood

Seven days later, the sky grew dark and the rain began. For forty days and forty nights, rain poured from the sky, and water burst from the ground. It covered the whole earth, rising higher than the tallest mountains (Genesis 7:17–20).

Everything and everyone outside the ark was swept away. But inside, Noah and his family were safe, surrounded by the sounds of animals and the creaking of the boat in the wind and waves (Genesis 7:23–24).

The Waters Recede — A New Beginning

After forty days, the rain stopped. But the water still covered the earth. Noah and his family waited patiently for the water to recede.

First, Noah sent out a raven, but it didn't bring back any sign of land. Then he sent a dove, and the dove returned with a fresh green leaf, proof that the waters were beginning to go back into the sea (Genesis 8:6–11).

Later, Noah sent out the dove again, and this time it didn't return. Soon, the ark came to rest on Mount Ararat, and God told Noah it was time to come out of the ark (Genesis 8:4, 15–17).

Noah, his family, and all the animals stepped onto dry ground and looked around at the world God had made clean.

Then, God made a covenant, a promise, that said, "Never again will I flood the whole earth" (Genesis 9:11).

Why This Story Matters

God saw how far people had turned from what was right, and His heart was grieved. But rather than treat everyone the same, He looked at each person individually, and He saw Noah. Though the world was full of evil, Noah stood out because of his good heart. He wasn't perfect, but he was faithful. God chose to use him for good.

God gave Noah some incredibly difficult tasks: build a massive ark, gather and care for the animals, and speak truth to people who did wrong. But Noah listened and obeyed in every situation. In response to Noah's faithfulness, God protected him and his family.

This story reminds us that even when the world feels loud, messy, or broken, God still sees each of us. We are not lost in the crowd. When we walk closely with Him each day, we will begin to hear His voice more clearly and understand the plan He has for our lives. No matter how big or impossible a task might seem, when we follow God in obedience and trust, *anything* is possible.

A Prayer to End

Dear God, thank You for Noah's story and for showing us what it means to trust You, even when life is difficult. Give us the same courage You gave Noah to do what is right, to build our lives on Your truth, and to not be swayed by the things of this world. Help us draw closer to You in prayer, through reading the Bible, and when we gather at church. Thank You for always having a plan and revealing it in Your perfect timing. And thank You for always keeping Your promises. Amen.

Bible References

Genesis 6:5–22 — God sees evil and instructs Noah
Genesis 7:1–24 — The flood begins, and the ark is sealed
Genesis 8:1–19 — The waters go down, and Noah leaves the ark
Genesis 9:1–17 — God's covenant and the rainbow

~ 2200 Years Before Christ (BC)

The Tower of Babel

God's Command to Go!

Many years after the flood, God gave Noah's family clear instructions to spread out across the earth, care for creation, and fill the land with life again (Genesis 9:1, 7). For a while, the people listened. They began to move to new places where they raised families, built homes, and explored the wide world that God had created for them. During this time, everyone still spoke the same language, which made it easy to work together and share ideas.

Shinar's Plan

But then, a group of people traveled eastward and decided to stop in a place called Shinar (Genesis 11:1–2). It was a rich land, full of open space and opportunity. Instead of continuing their journey like God commanded, they came up with their own idea. "Let's settle here," they said. "We'll build a city and a tower so tall that it touches the sky. People everywhere will know our name. We'll be famous. We won't need to go anywhere else" (Genesis 11:3–4).

Prideful Hearts

They wanted to feel strong and important, but instead of trusting God's plan, they trusted their own. They gathered clay, sand, straw, and water to make bricks. Then they used tar as mortar to hold everything together. They worked side by side, stacking the bricks carefully, raising the tower higher and higher. It was unlike anything the world had ever seen.

But their hearts began to change. They were not building to honor God; they were building to honor themselves. They wanted to be noticed, praised, and admired. The tower had become something like an idol, a symbol of human pride. They were trying to show the world that they could do great things without God, and maybe even reach heaven on their own.

They believed that by staying close together, they would be safer and stronger. But true strength cannot be found within crowds or tall buildings. True strength comes from trusting God, even when the path ahead is unknown. They wanted something they could control, something they could see with their eyes and touch with their hands. But God wanted their hearts.

God Steps in with Grace and Mercy

God saw what was happening in Shinar. He saw how the people were putting their own plans above His. He saw that their pride was pulling them further away from Him, and He knew that if they kept going this way, they would forget who He was and who they were made to be (Genesis 11:5–6).

So God stepped in, not out of anger, but out of love. Suddenly, everything changed. The people began speaking different languages (Genesis 11:7). Someone might ask, "Pass me another brick," but the person next to them could no longer understand. Confusion filled the air. Teams broke apart. Frustration grew. No one could continue the work.

The building stopped. The great tower was left unfinished. And from that moment on, the city became known as Babel, which means "confused," because that is where God changed their language and scattered them across the earth (Genesis 11:8–9). The people who had once been united in pride now went their separate ways, spreading out just as God had originally commanded.

God's Greater Plan

Some may have left Shinar feeling frustrated and disappointed that their tower remained incomplete. But God had protected them from something much worse: a life of false security, built on pride and human strength instead of faith in Him.

Even in the middle of that confusion, God was still working. He had a bigger plan, one that would eventually bring people from every nation and language back together, not to build a tower, but to become one family through Jesus. One day, people from all over the world would be united again, not by language, but by love and faith in the same Savior.

Why This Story Matters

This story reminds us that just because something is popular does not mean it is right. The people of Shinar ignored God's direction and chose their own plan. Maybe some of them knew it was not what God wanted. Did they speak up? Or did they stay quiet and follow the crowd?

The Tower of Babel also teaches us about pride. When we make choices without praying or thinking about what God wants, we are trusting in ourselves more than in Him. Are we doing things to glorify God or to make ourselves look good?

When we build our lives around our own ideas and leave God out, things start to fall apart. But when we follow His plan, He gives us peace, purpose, and blesses each of us. His ways are always better, even when we cannot see the full picture yet.

A Prayer to End

Dear God, in all that we do, help us build Your kingdom, and not ours. Keep our hearts humble and let our confidence come from You. When we feel lost or unsure, help us seek Your voice and wisdom above our own. We trust that You have a good plan for our lives. Please give us the patience and the ability to see it when it comes. Amen.

Bible References

Genesis 9:1, 7 — God commands Noah's family to multiply and fill the earth
Genesis 11:1–4 — The people decide to stay and build a tower in Shinar
Genesis 11:5–7 — God sees their pride and confuses their language
Genesis 11:8–9 — The people are scattered, and the city is named Babel

~ 2100 Years Before Christ (BC)

Abraham — The First Patriarch

A Promise Offered

Long after God commanded the people to scatter across the earth, a man was born through the family line of Noah's son, Shem, and became a key part of God's unfolding story. His name was Abram (Genesis 11:10–26).

God chose Abram to be the beginning of a promise, one that stretched across generations and reached people all over the world. Though he began as just one man in a small corner of the earth, God saw something in Abram's heart that pleased Him. Abram didn't yet know what God had planned, but one day, God spoke to him:

"Leave your country, your people, and your father's household, and go to the land I will show you. I will make you into a great nation … and all the families on earth will be blessed through you" (Genesis 12:1–3).

Abram's Faith Journey Begins

When God spoke to Abram, He didn't give him a map or explain what the land would look like. He simply said, "Go." With a faithful heart, Abram obeyed.

He gathered his wife Sarai, his nephew Lot, all their servants, and their possessions, and they began their journey. They traveled through deserts and unfamiliar lands, unsure of what would happen next, but they trusted God to protect them and provide the way.

As Abram prayed one clear and beautiful night, God took him outside and said, "Look at the stars. Count them if you can. That's how many descendants you will have" (Genesis 15:5).

Abram saw the massive number of stars as he gazed at the sky, but he still wondered, "When will this happen, Lord?"

The Lord's Promise to Abram

Abram continued to follow God and do all He asked. Because of his faithfulness, God blessed Abram with land, herds, and many people who served and supported his household. Despite the provision, Abram had questions about his family line becoming a great nation. He was nearly one hundred years old, and Sarai had never been able to have children.

Then God spoke again. "Walk with Me faithfully and be without fault, and I will make a promise to you. You will have many children, and they will become a great people. Through you, nations will be born" (Genesis 17:4–5).

At this, Abram fell to the ground in awe and worshiped. And God said, "From this day forward, your name will be Abraham, and your wife's name will be Sarah" (Genesis 17:15–16).

Not long after, Sarah became pregnant, just as God had promised.

Isaac Is Born; Abraham's Test

Sarah gave birth to a son. Both she and Abraham were very old, and it seemed impossible that she would deliver a baby so late in life. But with God, nothing is impossible (Genesis 21:1–7). Sarah laughed with joy, and they named the baby Isaac, which means "laughter."

When Isaac was still a young boy, God tested Abraham's faith. He told him to take Isaac on a journey, build an altar, and offer Isaac as a sacrifice (Genesis 22:1–2). This request broke Abraham's heart. He had waited so long for this child, and now God wanted to take Isaac back?

But Abraham trusted God. He believed that God would keep His promise, even if he couldn't understand how.

So, Abraham obeyed. He built the altar and prepared everything exactly as God asked. Just as he was about to give his son to God, the Lord called out, "Stop. Do not harm the boy" (Genesis 22:11–12). God had seen Abraham's faith. It was a test, and Abraham passed.

God provided a ram for the offering instead (Genesis 22:13–14). Abraham's trust had been proven, and the promise continued. Through Isaac, that promise eventually led to the birth of the Savior of the world.

Why This Story Matters

Abraham's story reminds us what trust really means. It means having faith in God's plans even when we don't fully understand what those plans are. It also reminds us that God is bigger than anything we could ever imagine. Abraham and Sarah didn't understand how they could become parents at such an old age. How many times do we face challenges in life that seem too big for even God to handle?

But the truth is, nothing is impossible for Him. When we bring our worries, fears, and questions to God, He listens, and He can do far more than we expect. The real question is, do we trust Him enough to believe that?

And just as important, this story reminds us to be patient. Abraham waited and waited for God's promises to come true. I'm sure there were moments when he felt unsure of the timing. But he never doubted *if* it would happen, only *when*. His faith was steady. So take heart: As our trust in God grows, so do the blessings He's preparing for us.

A Prayer to End

Dear God, thank You for the story of Abraham and the example of his faith. Help us to trust You the way he did, even when life feels uncertain. Teach us to be patient, to believe in Your promises, and to stay faithful no matter what. When things are hard or confusing, remind us that You are always working for good. Give us the wisdom and strength to make the right choices and to follow You every step of the way. Amen.

Bible References

Genesis 11:10–26 — The family line from Shem to Abram
Genesis 12:1–3 — God calls Abram to leave his home and follow Him
Genesis 15:5 — God promises Abram countless descendants
Genesis 17:4–5, 15–16 — God changes their names to Abraham and Sarah
Genesis 21:1–7 — Isaac is born
Genesis 22:1–14 — Abraham is tested and God provides a ram in place of Isaac

~ 2000 Years Before Christ (BC)

Jacob and Esau — A Birthright Taken

The Promise Passed to Isaac

God's promise of hope continued through Isaac, who grew up and married Rebekah. She was getting older and struggled to get pregnant. So, Isaac prayed earnestly for his wife to have a child. Eventually, God blessed her … not with just one baby but two. Twins!

While pregnant, her babies jostled each other within her womb as if they were wrestling with one another. Rebekah wondered, "Why is this happening to me?" The Lord said to her, "Two nations are in your womb … the older will serve the younger" (Genesis 25:22–23).

God's explanation foretold how these brothers' choices would shape their family's story for centuries. Esau would become the father of Edom, a nation that routinely lived in conflict with Israel, and Jacob would become the father of the Israelites, through whom Jesus came.

Brothers: The Adventurer and the Quiet Son

Esau was the firstborn. He was strong, hairy, and adventurous, and loved being outdoors. Like his father, Isaac, he loved to hunt and became skilled with a bow. He spent most of his time hunting in lush, wooded areas, seeking wild game to feed his family. His father loved Esau's wild, adventurous heart and favored him.

Jacob was born second. He came into the world holding onto Esau's heel, as if he were trying to pull his brother back because he knew the birthrights of the father went to the firstborn. This meant everything owned by the father — land, animals, servants, and other property — was given to the firstborn son through a special blessing that went into effect after the father passed away.

Jacob was a quiet boy who preferred to stay close to home, helping around the house, learning how to manage the family flocks, and growing very close with his mother, Rebekah, who favored him (Genesis 25:24–28).

Trading a Birthright for a Bowl of Stew

One afternoon, Esau came home starving after he'd been out hunting all day. He smelled the delicious stew Jacob made and had to have some. "Give me some of that stew!" Esau demanded. Jacob, always thinking two steps ahead of his brother, saw his opportunity. "First, sell me your birthright, your rights as the firstborn son," he said. Esau was so hungry, he didn't care. "What good is a birthright if I die of hunger?" he replied. So, he traded his inheritance, his blessing, for a bowl of stew (Genesis 25:29–34).

Jacob Steals Esau's Birthright

Many years later, Isaac, who was old and nearly blind, called out to his son Esau. He said, "I am not sure how much longer I will be with you, but with the time I do have here on earth, I would love to taste that wild game you're so good at making. Please, for your dear old dad, go hunt and prepare my favorite meal. Then I will give you my blessing (Genesis 27:1–4).

Rebekah overheard Isaac's intentions and didn't want Esau to receive his father's blessing because of God's promise to her: "The older will serve the younger." So, Rebekah came up with a plan. She told her younger son, Jacob, to choose the finest animal from the flock so she could cook one of Isaac's favorite meals. Then, she instructed Jacob to dress in his brother's hunting clothes and put goat skin, still covered with fur, on his arms and neck to make his body feel hairy like Esau's.

Wearing his costume, Jacob brought his father a meal and asked for his blessing. Isaac, whose sight had declined in his old age, was confused about who he was speaking to, Jacob or Esau. The person he touched felt and looked like Esau but sounded like Jacob. Eventually, Isaac decided that the son in front of him was Esau, so he mistakenly put his hands on Jacob and gave him his blessing. That act brought to life God's declaration to Rebekah: "The older will serve the younger" (Genesis 27:5–29).

Esau's Anger — And Jacob's Planned Escape

When Esau returned home with the meal for his father and found out what Jacob had done, he was angry. "Jacob stole my blessing!" he cried. Esau was so enraged that he threatened to kill Jacob on the spot (Genesis 27:30–41).

Out of fear, Rebekah made plans for Jacob to flee for safety to his uncle's house in a faraway land. Jacob was devastated; he'd have to leave Rebekah and the family home he grew up in.

Both brothers were heartbroken by their decisions, and now they were separated by a great distance that caused their family to be torn apart. But even in this mess, God planned for something special to come from Jacob's time in Harran, his uncle's homeland (Genesis 27:42–45).

Why This Story Matters

In a single moment, Esau gave up something lasting and meaningful for something temporary and unimportant. He didn't stop to think through his actions or his words. Instead, he made a hasty decision without seeking God or the wise counsel of others. His story reminds us that every choice we make, whether big or small, matters.

Rebekah also received a promise. God told her that Jacob, her younger son, would be greater than his brother. But instead of trusting God to fulfill that promise in His own time and way, Rebekah took matters into her own hands. She devised a plan to trick Isaac so that Jacob would receive the blessing. Her plotting deeply divided the family and tore it apart.

This story teaches us that it is not enough to just *know* God's plan; we must also trust Him with the *how* and *when*. When we try to force the outcome we want, even with good intentions, we often cause pain and confusion. But when we follow God's timing and seek His will and guidance every step of the way, we're confident that His plans will unfold in the right way, at the right time.

A Prayer to End

Dear God, help us turn away from the temporary things of this world and focus on what is eternal. Give us the wisdom to know the difference between the two. Teach us to speak truthfully and kindly, never spreading lies, rumors, or judgment toward others. We know Your timing is always perfect. Help us be patient and ready to receive Your plans with grateful hearts. And while we wait, keep us from trying to control situations or force outcomes of our own. Instead, teach us to trust that Your way is always best. Amen.

Bible References

Genesis 25:22–23 — God tells Rebekah two nations are in her womb
Genesis 25:24–28 — Esau and Jacob are born
Genesis 25:29–34 — Esau sells his birthright for stew
Genesis 27:1–4 — Isaac plans to bless Esau
Genesis 27:5–29 — Jacob disguises himself and receives the blessing
Genesis 27:30–41 — Esau returns and reacts in anger
Genesis 27:42–45 — Rebekah urges Jacob to flee for safety

Joseph — From Favorite Son to Betrayed Brother

The Family in Harran

God blessed everything Jacob did in Harran. While he stayed there, he worked for his uncle as a shepherd for about 20 years. The flocks Jacob looked after grew quickly and brought great prosperity to his uncle and, later in life, himself. God also blessed Jacob with children, including twelve boys whose names represented the twelve tribes of Israel. In birth order, his sons' names were: Reuben, Simeon, Levi, Judah, Dan, Naphtali, Gad, Asher, Issachar, Zebulun, Joseph, and Benjamin (Genesis 29:31–35; 30:1–24; 35:16–18).

Betrayal in the Fields

Of all Jacob's sons, he loved Joseph the most. Rachel, Jacob's beloved second wife, gave birth to Joseph much later in Jacob's life. He was their firstborn and was special in their eyes. Jacob showed his fondness for his son by giving him a beautiful coat with bright colors. Upon seeing their father do this, Joseph's brothers hated him, and they became very jealous (Genesis 37:3–4).

Joseph's Dreams of What's to Come

One day, Joseph told his brothers about a dream he had. He said to them, "We were putting bundles of grain together out in the field, and suddenly my bundle stood upright while your bundles gathered around mine and bowed down to it" (Genesis 37:5–7).

His brothers understood exactly what he meant and said to him, "Do you think you will really rule over us?" Another night, Joseph explained another dream to his father and his brothers. He said, "I had another dream, and this time the sun and moon and eleven stars were bowing down to me" (Genesis 37:9).

His father laughed, "Do you really think your mother and I and your eleven brothers will actually come and bow down to you?" His brothers were jealous of him, but his father kept what Joseph said in mind (Genesis 37:10–11).

A Selfish Plan — Betrayed in the Fields

One day, Jacob asked Joseph to check on his brothers, who were tending to the family herds far away from their home in Canaan. During his journey, a man found him wandering around and asked him what he was looking for. Joseph said he was searching for his brothers, and the man told him where he could find them (Genesis 37:13–17).

His brothers saw Joseph from far away because his colorful coat glistened in the sun. They began to plot against him. "Here comes the dreamer," they said. "Come now, let's kill him. Then we'll see what becomes of his dreams" (Genesis 37:18–20).

At first, they plotted to kill him, but his brother Reuben convinced the group to throw Joseph into a dry water well instead, secretly hoping to rescue him later when his brothers were asleep. When Joseph reached his brothers, they stripped him of his robe and tossed him into the well (Genesis 37:21–24).

Sold as a Slave

After this happened, the brothers sat together to eat lunch and revel in what they had just done. Then, in the distance, they saw a caravan of traders carrying spices and grains as they headed to Egypt to conduct business. Judah said to his brothers, "What will we gain if we kill our brother? Let's sell him. After all, he is our brother" (Genesis 37:25–27).

So, the traders came by where Joseph's brothers were gathered, and they sold him as a slave for twenty pieces of silver. Then, they took his beautiful coat, ripped it, and covered it in goat's blood. When they returned home, they gave the bloodied coat to their father and lied, saying, "A wild animal killed him" (Genesis 37:28–32).

Jacob immediately recognized the coat as the one he had given to the son he loved the most. He wept bitterly, believing Joseph was gone forever (Genesis 37:33–35).

Meanwhile, Joseph felt angry, scared, and betrayed by his family and was on his way to Egypt with a group of traders he did not know. But even though he was physically alone, God was with him (Genesis 37:36).

Why This Story Matters

Joseph's story reminds us that when jealousy is left unchecked, it can cause us to make hurtful decisions, even toward those who love us most. Anger and bitterness are signals that something in our hearts is out of alignment, and those feelings give us a chance to pause, pray, and seek God's help to set things right.

But this story also shows that nothing or no one can stop God's plans. When Joseph left home to check on his brothers, he didn't know where to find them. Yet a stranger appeared, saw him wandering, and pointed him in the right direction. Then, when his brothers grew enraged and plotted to kill him, Reuben spoke up and convinced them to spare Joseph's life … so they threw him down a well instead.

God worked through every twist in Joseph's journey. His constant care and protection reveal that God's purpose will always prevail. Even when life feels unfair or broken, we can trust that God is still moving behind the scenes, shaping our story for something greater.

A Prayer to End

Dear God, help us understand how harmful jealousy and envy can be when they take root in our hearts. Teach us to build healthy, loving relationships with our siblings and friends, and when those relationships are tested, give us the wisdom, patience, and courage to make things right. Remind us not to compare ourselves to others, but to see ourselves through Your loving eyes. And when life feels unfair, help us trust that You are always at work, shaping our stories for Your purpose and glory. Amen.

Bible References

Genesis 29:31–35; 30:1–24; 35:16–18 — Jacob's sons are born
Genesis 37:3–4 — Jacob gives Joseph a colorful coat
Genesis 37:5–11 — Joseph shares his dreams
Genesis 37:13–20 — Joseph searches for his brothers, and they plot against him
Genesis 37:21–24 — Reuben tries to protect Joseph
Genesis 37:25–28 — Joseph is sold to traders
Genesis 37:29–35 — Jacob mourns
Genesis 37:36 — Joseph is taken to Egypt

~ 1900 – 1800 Years Before Christ (BC)

Joseph — From Slave to Merciful Leader

From Slave to Steward Over Egypt

Once Joseph arrived in Egypt, the traders sold him in a market as a slave to Potiphar. Potiphar was the captain of the guard, an entrusted official who served the Pharaoh, the king of Egypt. Joseph immediately went to work within the household of his new master, and God blessed everything Joseph did. Potiphar left everything he possessed in Joseph's care after seeing God's favor toward him. With Joseph in charge, Potiphar did not concern himself with anything except the food he ate (Genesis 39:1–6).

When Potiphar's wife saw Joseph's success, she desired him, but he denied her advances. In response, she lied and told Potiphar that Joseph made advances toward her. After hearing this, Potiphar threw Joseph in jail to be forgotten, once again (Genesis 39:7–20).

From Prisoner to Leader

Soon after being placed in jail, the captain of the guard realized that God was with Joseph and put him in charge of the entire prison (Genesis 39:21–23). One day, while making his rounds, Joseph noticed two prisoners who were visibly upset. After inquiring, Joseph learned both prisoners had dreams that neither was able to interpret. After telling Joseph, over the next few days, their dreams came true just as he described (Genesis 40:1–23).

Two years later, the King of Egypt also had a disturbing dream. He stood by the Nile River and saw seven fat cows come out of the river. Then, seven skinny cows came out and stood beside those already on the riverbank (Genesis 41:1–4).

The king did not understand the dream, so he called his royal subjects together to inquire if someone could explain what he had seen. But no one could. Soon, word spread that there was a prisoner who could decipher dreams. The king summoned Joseph, who cleaned up, put on new clothes, and came before Pharaoh. Pharaoh probed, "I heard that you can interpret dreams. If so, listen carefully and tell me what it means." Joseph replied, "I cannot do it, but God will give Pharaoh the answer he desires" (Genesis 41:14–16). Then, he listened carefully as Pharaoh described the dream. After hearing the details, Joseph spoke with confidence, "Pharaoh, God is showing you what is coming, seven years of plenty, followed by seven years of famine" (Genesis 41:28–30).

Pharaoh was amazed at Joseph's abilities and knew that God was with him. He said, "You will be second in command over all Egypt. Only I will be greater than you" (Genesis 41:39–41).

In that moment, Joseph went from a prisoner to a ruler, just as God planned.

The Famine — A Family Reunited

For the next seven years of abundance, Joseph took charge and directed all of Egypt to give one-fifth of their harvest as an offering to Pharaoh. Joseph stored the food in warehouses built in Egypt (Genesis 41:47–49), and people came from all over the region to buy food.

Back in Canaan, food ran low, so to prevent their starvation, Jacob told his sons to travel to Egypt to secure some grain (Genesis 42:1–2). After a long, hard journey, the brothers finally reached one of Egypt's largest food warehouses, the one Joseph managed. They did not recognize their brother when they arrived. Joseph was dressed as an Egyptian ruler when he stood in front of them. Even though they didn't recognize him, Joseph knew exactly who they were. They immediately fell to their knees and bowed to him as he approached them, just like in his dreams (Genesis 42:6–9).

Joseph could have punished them for the pain they caused him all those years ago, but he chose to forgive them instead. With tears streaming down his face, he told them the truth, "I am Joseph, your brother, the one you sold into Egypt. But do not be afraid. What you meant for harm, God meant for good, to save many lives" (Genesis 50:20).

Joseph, still weeping, welcomed his brothers to Egypt and sent for his father Jacob to join them, where they would be safe (Genesis 45:3–11).

A Blessed Life in Egypt

Under Joseph's leadership and those who followed, the Israelites flourished in Egypt for hundreds of years. But things changed when another Pharaoh came to power who knew nothing of Joseph or his God (Exodus 1:6–8).

The Israelites became slaves under the new Pharaoh, and after God heard their desperate pleas, He sent a man to rescue them. That is where the next story begins.

Why This Story Matters

Joseph's heart was in the right place, which is why he could forgive his brothers. He didn't let anger and bitterness seep into his heart and change his outlook on life, even when it was hard and painful. When we trust God's plan and allow Him to transform our hearts, we begin to see the purpose He has for our lives more clearly. That clarity gives us strength and hope to endure the seasons of struggle that come along the way.

When Pharaoh told Joseph, "I heard you can interpret dreams," Joseph didn't say, "Yeah, I'm pretty special. I can do that." No, he gave God the rightful credit and let Pharaoh know that He was behind his success. We honor God when we use the gifts and talents He gives us and proclaim that He, not us, deserves the glory.

A Prayer to End

Dear God, thank You for showing us through Joseph's story what true faith and forgiveness look like. Help us remember that Your plans cannot be changed and that they are always working for our good. Teach us to praise Your name in both the good and difficult times. Help us stay confident yet humble, never insecure or prideful. And if we are ever placed in a position of leadership or authority, guide us to be fair, honest, and kind to those we serve. Thank You for always being faithful to Your people, then and now. Amen

Bible References

Genesis 39:1–6 — Joseph is sold to Potiphar and given charge of the household

Genesis 39:7–20 — Joseph is falsely accused and sent to prison

Genesis 39:21–23 — Joseph is put in charge of the prison

Genesis 40:1–23 — Joseph interprets dreams in prison

Genesis 41:1–41 — Joseph interprets Pharaoh's dream and is made second in command

Genesis 41:47–49 — Joseph stores food during years of plenty

Genesis 42:1–9 — Joseph's brothers come to Egypt for food

Genesis 45:3–11 — Joseph reveals himself and invites Jacob to Egypt

Genesis 50:20 — "What you meant for harm, God meant for good"

Exodus 1:6–8 — A new Pharaoh forgets Joseph and enslaves the Israelites

DECEMBER 10

~ 1530 – 1440 Years Before Christ (BC)

The Exodus from Egypt

Israel Enslaved

The new Pharaoh feared that this growing nation of people would rise to power and take over Egypt. To control them, he forced the entire Israelite population into slavery, treating them poorly and working them hard. Additionally, to curtail the size of the Israelite population, he commanded that every Hebrew newborn boy be thrown into the Nile River (Exodus 1:6–22).

The Baby in the Basket

However, one mother refused to follow Pharaoh's decree. She kept her newborn at home for three months, but as the baby grew, she realized there was no way to keep him hidden without someone noticing. So, she decided to put the infant into a waterproofed wicker basket that she placed in the Nile River. She prayed that God would keep the basket afloat long enough for someone to find it downstream (Exodus 2:2–3).

Miriam, the baby's sister, watched from afar as the river took the basket toward the Pharaoh's daughter, where she was bathing. When she saw the beautiful baby boy in the basket, she felt sorry for him, because she knew he belonged to an Israelite mother who was forced to give him up (Exodus 2:4–6).

As she admired the baby, Miriam approached Pharaoh's daughter and offered to find someone to care for the child. That someone was the child's biological mother! Miriam intervened so her mom could help nurture him before he was raised as a prince in Pharaoh's palace (Exodus 2:7–9).

Moses Flees to Midian

Pharaoh's daughter eagerly named her new son Moses. And even though He was trained in all the ways of an Egyptian prince, he always sensed his Israelite heritage and was upset to see how the Egyptians treated his people. One day, he came across an Egyptian guard beating a slave, and in a fit of anger, struck and killed the guard (Exodus 2:10–12).

When Pharaoh heard the news about Moses' actions, Moses feared for his life and fled to a desert region. He lived in a town called Midian and worked as a shepherd (Exodus 2:15). But God had bigger plans for him.

The Burning Bush

While tending his sheep one day, Moses noticed a bush on fire, but it didn't burn up! As he stepped closer, he heard God's voice: "Moses! Take off your sandals, for you are standing on holy ground." God told Moses, "I have seen My people suffer. Go to Pharaoh and tell him, 'Let My people go!'" (Exodus 3:1–10).

Moses was afraid. "What if he won't listen?" "I will be with you," God promised, and then showed Moses miracles to demonstrate His power. He also let Moses' brother, Aaron, help him (Exodus 4:1–17).

Let My People Go!

Moses and Aaron stood before Pharaoh. "The Lord says, 'Let My people go!'" Moses declared. Pharaoh laughed. "I will not let them go!" (Exodus 5:1–2).

So, through Moses, God sent ten plagues to show His power to Pharaoh and the Egyptians (Exodus 7–11).

1. The Nile turned to blood
2. Frogs covered the land
3. Gnats filled the air
4. Swarms of flies
5. Livestock died
6. Painful Boils
7. Hail and fire rained from the sky
8. Locusts ate the crops
9. Darkness covered Egypt
10. The firstborn of each family died

Pharaoh begged for relief after each plague, and God granted it. But Pharaoh's heart grew hard; he repeatedly went back on his word and refused to let God's people go. Before God sent the final plague — the death of the firstborn — He gave the Israelites a way to escape death: He commanded them to sacrifice a lamb without any defects and smear its blood around the front door of their home. That night, God's angel of death came down from heaven and passed over every house that had blood painted on the door, sparing the life of each firstborn inside. On the other hand, all the Egyptian firstborn sons and daughters died, including Pharaoh's son. His death finally convinced Pharaoh to give in. "Go! Take your people and leave, now!" The Israelites later celebrated this miraculous event as the Passover, because the angel of death passed over each Israelite's home (Exodus 12:1–31).

Free at Last

The Israelites hurried out of Egypt, but Pharaoh changed his mind again about letting them go and chased after them (Exodus 14:5–9). They were trapped: the Red Sea ahead, Pharaoh's army behind. But Moses encouraged them, "Do not be afraid. Watch what God will do!" Then, he lifted his staff, and the Red Sea split in two! The Israelites rushed across on dry ground. When Pharaoh's army followed, the water crashed back down and swept them away (Exodus 14:21–28).

The Israelites cheered; they were truly free! God used Moses to lead His people out of slavery, but their journey to a new land was just beginning.

Why This Story Matters

Moses grew up in a palace with comfort and power, but something in his heart pulled him in a different direction. He knew God was calling him to step away from the life he had always known and to stand up for his people. After fleeing, he still felt for those he left behind. God saw his heart and faithfulness and gave him the strength to do something about it.

In our own lives, we may find ourselves in situations we know are not right, but we feel unsure how to change them. Maybe the people around us are making poor choices, someone in need keeps getting ignored, or we've made a mistake that feels impossible to fix.

Moses' story reminds us that there is no situation too broken for God to step into. When we bring our weaknesses, worries, and fears to Him, He will listen. He will guide us. And He will show up in our time of need.

A Prayer to End

Dear God, give us the confidence and courage to do the right thing even in the face of overwhelming adversity. Open our eyes to see the needs of those around us who are less fortunate than we are, and guide us to act through Your strength and compassion. Thank You for hearing the cries of Your people and for showing up in powerful and faithful ways. Amen.

Bible References

Exodus 1:6–22 — Israelites are enslaved, and Pharaoh decrees the killing of newborn boys
Exodus 2:1–10 — Moses is hidden in a basket and adopted by Pharaoh's daughter
Exodus 2:11–15 — Moses kills an Egyptian and flees to Midian
Exodus 3:1–10 — The burning bush and God's call to Moses
Exodus 4:1–17 — God equips Moses and sends Aaron
Exodus 5:1–2 — Moses tells Pharaoh to let God's people go
Exodus 7–11 — The ten plagues of Egypt
Exodus 12:1–30 — The Passover and death of the firstborn
Exodus 14:5–28 — The parting of the Red Sea and Israel's deliverance

DECEMBER 11

~ 1450 – 1405 Years Before Christ (BC)

Moses Leads the Israelites
into the Wilderness

God Provides, but His People Grumble

Now finally free, God promised the Israelites a new home called the Promised Land. This area was a good and fertile land, also known as the land of "milk and honey" (Exodus 3:8). But getting to this new land wouldn't be easy. The people would have to walk through a hot, dry, and dangerous desert. Soon, when this reality set in, the people started to complain.

"If only we had died by the Lord's hand in Egypt! There we sat around pots of meat and ate all the food we wanted, but you have brought us out into this desert to starve all of us to death" (Exodus 16:3).

But God provided for His people every day. Each evening, He sent quail down to their camp for dinner, and each morning He'd send manna, a type of bread from heaven, for breakfast (Exodus 16:11–15). When they needed water to drink, He made springs of water flow from a rock (Exodus 17:6). Even though God continued to bless the people, they still doubted He would provide. Their attitudes and lack of belief frustrated Moses, but the people continued to follow him into the Desert of Sinai, where God had something important to tell them (Exodus 19:1).

Mount Sinai —The Commandment Tablets Broken

God called Moses up to the mountain and said, "If you obey me fully and keep my covenant, then out of all nations you will be my treasured possession" (Exodus 19:5). When Moses came down to speak to the elders about what God had shared, the people responded together, "We will do everything the Lord has said" (Exodus 19:8).

Moses brought back the people's answer to the Lord.

Next, God spoke the Ten Commandments to him, which were engraved on two stone tablets. These rules outlined how people were to love God and to love each other (Exodus 20:1–17; Exodus 24:12). Living in slavery under Pharaoh, the Israelites forgot how to live as a free people, so God gave them these commands as both a moral and societal guide. They were not just spiritual rules, but a way to create a just and holy nation. But while Moses was with God on the mountain, the people grew impatient and muttered, "Where's Moses? Did he leave us? We need a new god to lead us!" (Exodus 32:1).

Worship of the Golden Calf

Moses' brother Aaron gave the people what they wanted. While Moses was on the mountain with God, the people gave Aaron all their gold, and with his own hands, he melted it and made a golden calf. Immediately, the people started to sing, dance, and pray, "This is the god that saved us from Egypt!" (Exodus 32:2–4).

In a brief moment of fear, the people abandoned their true God. Moses' heart sank when he returned and saw the people worshiping the false god. He threw the stone tablets down in anger, and they shattered (Exodus 32:19). He then destroyed the golden calf and told the Israelites they had committed a great sin. They would endure consequences since the people turned away from God (Exodus 32:20–35).

Tent of Meeting

Moses pitched a tent some distance from camp and called it the Tent of Meeting, where he spoke to God face-to-face, as one speaks to a friend (Exodus 33:7–11). There, he apologized for the people's actions. God forgave them because of His favor toward Moses, a man who loved God with all his heart. While there, Moses asked for wisdom and for God's presence to be with them as the Israelites continued their journey to the Promised Land (Exodus 33:12–14). God then asked Moses to chisel out two new stone tablets and join Him on top of Mount Sinai the next day (Exodus 34:1–2).

Ten Commandments Rewritten

The next morning, Moses hiked up Mount Sinai with the stone tablets. There, God passed in front of Moses, who bowed down at once and worshiped the Lord (Exodus 34:4–8). God said, "Obey what I command you today" (Exodus 34:11). Moses stayed with the Lord for forty days and forty nights and during that time wrote the words of the covenant, the Ten Commandments, on the tablets (Exodus 34:28).

1. Thou shall not have any other Gods but me
2. Thou shall not use the Lord's name in vain
3. Thou shall keep the Sabbath day Holy
4. Thou shall honor your father and mother
5. Thou shall not kill
6. Thou shall not commit adultery
7. Thou shall not steal
8. Thou shall not lie about your neighbor
9. Thou shall not want your neighbor's wife
10. Thou shall not envy your neighbor's things

Forty Years in the Desert

After much turmoil and many mistakes, the Israelites finally reached the edge of the Promised Land. But their lack of faith continued, so God confused them and caused the Israelites to wander in the desert for forty years (Numbers 14:33–34). He did not allow any of the adults to enter the Promised Land, except two faithful men, Joshua and Caleb (Numbers 14:30). Moses, before his death, chose Joshua to be the new leader, and he encouraged the people with this truth, "Be strong and courageous! Do not be afraid, for the Lord your God is with you" (Deuteronomy 31:6). With that declaration, they moved one step closer to claim the land God had promised them.

Why This Story Matters

This story reminds us of the importance of being grounded in our faith. The Israelites' trust in God often wavered depending on their circumstances. When life was good, they praised Him. When life became difficult, they quickly turned away. Their desire to take control of their own situation often delayed the very outcomes God intended for them.

When things don't go our way, we often do the same. We plan, fix, and try to solve problems on our own. But when we fail to seek God's guidance first, our challenges often grow heavier. Even when we mess up, complain, doubt, or run ahead of Him, God remains near, patiently waiting for us to return and seek His direction.

We also see that God is the ultimate provider. In the wilderness, He gave His people food and water each day, teaching them to depend on Him instead of themselves. His hope was that they would come to Him daily, trust Him to provide, and learn to place their confidence in the Maker of Heaven and Earth.

The same is true today. God provides exactly what we need, and no more. When our hearts are not in the right place, having more than we need can make us forget that we still depend on Him. So, in His wisdom, He gives us just enough to remind us to seek Him every day and stay close to Him.

A Prayer to End

Dear God, thank You for being patient with us even though we're not perfect. Thank You for providing exactly what we need each day and reminding us that Your provision is always enough. When we grow weary or begin to doubt ourselves, teach us to trust in You always. And give us the courage and faith to follow You, wherever You lead us. Amen.

Bible References

Exodus 3 — God promises to rescue His people and bring them to a land of milk and honey

Exodus 16–17 — God provides manna, quail, and water from a rock

Exodus 19–20 — God speaks to Moses and gives the Ten Commandments

Exodus 32–34 — The golden calf and Moses' anger. Moses meets with God in the Tent; tablets made

Numbers 14 — Israelites doubt and wander for forty years

Deuteronomy 31 — Moses gives leadership to Joshua and encourages the people

~ 1400 Years Before Christ (BC)

Battle of Jericho

The Spies are Sent Out

After Moses died, the Lord said to Joshua, "Moses my servant is dead. Now you will lead my people across the Jordan River into the land I promised … be careful to obey all the commandments my servant Moses gave you, so that you may be successful wherever you go" (Joshua 1:1–9). Joshua prepared his people and secretly sent two spies to Jericho to check out the land (Joshua 2:1).

The spies snuck into Jericho through the main city gate. Soon, the king of Jericho got word that spies had entered the city, so he sent men out to look for them. As the spies went through the city, they spotted guards in the marketplace who were searching for them. Hoping to stay hidden and to get off the streets quickly, they found refuge with a woman named Rahab, who welcomed them into her home (Joshua 2:1).

The king heard that the spies had visited Rahab's house and sent her a message asking her to bring the men out. She explained that they came to see her but had already departed. When the king's guards arrived, she misdirected them by taking the group outside the city, pointing the way in which the men supposedly escaped. After the guards left, Rahab went to the roof and uncovered the spies, who hid underneath a pile of hay (Joshua 2:2–6).

She said, "I know the Lord has given you this land. Now please, swear to me that when you come to take this city you will show me and my family the same kindness I showed you" (Joshua 2:9–12). The spies agreed and instructed her to tie a scarlet cord around her window to ensure that everyone inside her home would be spared from death (Joshua 2:17–21). The spies then climbed out the window, lowered themselves with a rope, and returned to Joshua and the rest of the people.

God Provides a Way Across the Jordan

Before they arrived at Jericho, Joshua and the people had to cross the Jordan River, which was wide, deep, and moving fast. How would they get across? At God's command, Joshua ordered the priests to carry the Ark of the Covenant into the river. The river completely stopped flowing as soon as the priests' feet touched the water, allowing the Israelites to cross on dry ground (Joshua 3:13–17).

The Battle Plan

Joshua gathered the Israelite army and gave them their orders: "We won't fight this battle the way they expect. Instead, we will march around the city once a day for six days. The priests will blow their trumpets, but no one else is to say a word" (Joshua 6:3–4).

The people listened carefully but thought to themselves, "March? I thought we were going to battle?"

Joshua continued, "On the seventh day, we will march seven times. Then, when I give the command, we will blow the trumpets and shout, and the walls will fall" (Joshua 6:5). It sounded like a strange plan, but the Israelites had seen God do the impossible. If He said the wall would fall, then they believed Him!

The Faithful March

Early the next morning, the Israelites left camp for Jericho. The strongest led the way, followed by priests carrying the Ark of the Covenant. Thousands of Israelites marched in unison, in complete silence, with trumpets making the only sound (Joshua 6:6–9).

Inside the city of Jericho, the people looked down from the wall and laughed. "What are they doing?" one man scoffed. "Marching won't do anything!" But the Israelites kept marching.

One day passed, followed by another. Then another. Every morning, the same sight, a huge silent army circling the city. Then on the seventh day, the Israelites circled the city seven times. On the final lap, Joshua raised his voice. "Shout! For the Lord has given you this city!" (Joshua 6:16). Together the Israelites shouted with all their might. And before their eyes, the walls of Jericho crumbled to the ground.

The city that seemed too big to defeat was now open before them. God kept His promise (Joshua 6:20).

Why This Story Matters

The two spies Joshua sent to Jericho would surely be captured, but God used Rahab to save them. The Jordan River seemed impossible to cross, but God stopped the river and allowed the Israelites to cross on dry ground. There was no way a wall could come crumbling down by circling it and shouting at it, but it fell. These events didn't happen because the Israelites used their strength or weapons. They came true because God's people listened, obeyed, and trusted that He would lead them every step of the way.

The story of Jericho and Joshua reminds us that the road to victory doesn't always come the way we expect. Sometimes God's plans are hard to understand, and the obstacles ahead may seem impossible, but when we open our hearts to Him — listening, trusting, and obeying — His power shows up in incredible ways.

A Prayer to End

Dear God, thank You for showing us Joshua's example of what true courage and faith to follow You looks like. Help us to trust in You, as he did, even when Your plans don't make sense to us. Help us remember that with You, we can face any situation, no matter how big or small, because You are always there, right by our side. Amen.

Bible References

Joshua 1 — God commissions Joshua to lead Israel
Joshua 2 — Rahab hides the spies and makes a covenant
Joshua 3 — The Jordan River is parted
Joshua 6 — God's instructions and the fall of Jericho

DECEMBER 13

~ 1375 – 1050 Years Before Christ (BC)

The Time of the Judges

Long after Moses led the Israelites out of Egypt and after Joshua brought them into the Promised Land, God commanded them to remove the Canaanites from the region. He gave them this order because of the evil things these people had done; He didn't want the Israelites to live next to the Canaanites and pick up their customs or religious traditions (Judges 2:1–3). But the Israelites did not follow all of God's commands (Judges 1:27–28).

At first, the twelve tribes of Israel settled in the designated lands God promised them. For a time, everything seemed good. The Israelites prospered and lived in areas full of rich soil for farming and green pastures for building their homes. But they did not obey the Ten Commandments nor look to God for answers. Instead, the judges and leaders allowed the people to practice the Canaanites' religious customs. The Israelites worshiped the false gods of other nations and became morally corrupt (Judges 2:10–13). Just like that, they drifted further and further away from the God who loved them most.

Who Were the Judges?

In all, God chose twelve judges to help the Israelites with the impending dangers they faced over a period of three hundred years. These judges each came from one of the twelve tribes of Israel, but they didn't lead the entire nation.

You may be familiar with some of their names:

- Deborah, a strong and fearless woman who led the Israelites into battle when no one else would (Judges 4:4–10).
- Gideon, who was scared to lead at first but over time learned to trust God and led three hundred men to defeat a huge army (Judges 6–7).
- Samson, a man gifted with incredible strength and power, but who often forgot where his strength truly came from (Judges 13–16).

A Terrible Cycle — Forgetting and Remembering

The book of Judges tells story after story that repeat themselves, like a spinning wheel. They go something like this:

Initially, the people lived the life God intended, then they turned their backs on Him and chose sin, idol worship, and selfish living. God allowed neighboring enemies to come into their lands and conquer them (Judges 2:14–15). When the conquering army devastated the Israelites' lives, the people remembered God again. They cried out, "God, help us!" and God heard them every single time (Judges 2:16–18).

God sent judges, leaders He chose, to intervene and save His people. These judges were far from perfect. Some were brave warriors, some were cowards, some were wise, and some made plenty of mistakes. But God chose each one of them to rescue the Israelites and remind them that He still fought for them. Once His people were saved, the land remained peaceful for a time. The people remembered God, were obedient, and followed His ways again. Then slowly, little by little, the cycle of sin, idol worship, and selfish living started all over again.

Electing a King

The book of Judges ends with one final haunting sentence:

"In those days, Israel had no king; everyone did what was right in their own eyes" (Judges 21:25).

Without a good judge to lead them, the people went their own way and ended up miserable, lost, and broken. They needed someone to guide them as Moses had … calling them out to live the full lives God planned for them and encouraging them to follow the commandments and love their neighbor.

The Israelites needed a stronger relationship with God. Unfortunately, they asked for an elected king to rule over them so Israel would look like other successful nations that were also led by kings (1 Samuel 8:4–5).

Why This Story Matters

The Book of Judges can be difficult to read. It features people who made bad choices, but it's also a story of God's endless mercy and forgiveness. No matter how many times the Israelites turned away from God, He waited for them. Each time they asked for help, He heard them. Each time they needed someone to rescue them, He sent help.

And guess what? God is still the same today. He never changes. In life, we might mess up in big ways, get involved in other things, and totally forget about Him. It doesn't matter. The moment we decide to turn back to Him and say, "God, I need You in my life," He hears us and is already in our presence, waiting with open arms for us to come back to Him.

A Prayer to End

Dear God, thank You for loving us even though we are not perfect and make mistakes. Thank You for never giving up on us, even when we forget or give up on You. Help us be more consistent in our faith and break the downward cycle of sin and disobedience that plagued the time of Judges. Teach us to trust in You every day and to follow Your ways with grateful hearts. Amen.

Bible References

Judges 1–2 — Israel fails to drive out Canaanites; the cycle of sin begins

Judges 4–5 — Deborah leads Israel

Judges 6–7 — Gideon defeats the Midianites

Judges 13–16 — Samson's life and battles

Judges 21:25 — "Everyone did what was right in their own eyes."

1 Samuel 8 — Israel asks for a king

DECEMBER 14

~ 1100 Years Before Christ (BC)

Ruth's Story — Loyalty and Love

Famine and Loss in a Foreign Land

There was a great famine across the land during the days when the judges still ruled Israel. A family from Bethlehem decided to take their chances in the nation of Moab with the hopes of finding a better life. So the man, Elimelek, his wife Naomi, and their sons Mahlon and Kilion, packed all they had and left their home and family property behind (Ruth 1:1–2).

Soon after they arrived, Naomi's husband died, and she was left with only her two sons. Later, both of her sons married Moabite women named Orpah and Ruth. Then, after living in Moab for ten years, Naomi's sons died (Ruth 1:3–5). So, she made the decision to travel back to Bethlehem with her two daughters-in-law after hearing the great stories of God's provision for the Israelites.

But Naomi had a change of heart and decided it would be best for Orpah and Ruth to stay in Moab and start a new life. She wanted to spare them the hardships she knew they'd face in Bethlehem because of the history between the two nations (Deuteronomy 23:3–4).

Ruth's Remarkable Devotion

Naomi said to Orpah and Ruth, "Go back, each of you, to your mother's home." Then she kissed them goodbye, and they wept aloud and said to her, "We will go back with you to your people." Naomi insisted they return to their homes for a better life. Orpah obeyed, kissed Naomi, and left. However, Ruth clung to Naomi and said, with tears in her eyes, words so powerful that they are often quoted today:

"Where you go, I will go. Where you stay, I will stay. Your people will be my people, and your God will be my God" (Ruth 1:16–17).

Ruth walked away from everything she knew to become a stranger in a strange land. She also knew that she was heading to a nation that looked down on Moabites, lessening her chances of finding a new husband. But Ruth stayed faithful, not just to Naomi, but also to God. She trusted that Naomi's God, the God of Israel, would be her God too.

God Provides

Ruth and Naomi arrived in Bethlehem with no money, no jobs, and nowhere to live. But God was already at work to provide for them both. Early one morning, Ruth gathered leftover grain from a field. To provide for the poor, there was a law that required farmers not to harvest all the grain, but leave some behind for those in need (Leviticus 19:9–10; Ruth 2:2–3).

While in the fields, Ruth caught the eye of Boaz, a kind and godly man who owned the property where she worked. Boaz was a distant relative of Naomi's. Through their shared family, he heard about Ruth's boldness and faithfulness toward Naomi and others in Bethlehem (Ruth 2:10–12). Boaz cared for Ruth, so to ensure her safety, he allowed her to take as much food from his fields as she could carry (Ruth 2:15–16). Over time, God weaved their story together in a way that no one could have imagined.

Boaz's Commitment as the Family Redeemer

Back in the day, it was the responsibility of the closest male family member to care for the living widow of another family member and redeem them. Boaz served as Naomi's redeemer and stepped forward to help her and Ruth. He also bought the property that Naomi's husband, Elimelek, owned (Ruth 4:3–10).

A Legacy that Leads to Jesus

After Boaz redeemed Naomi and became responsible for her family, he married Ruth. Their story of amazing love and faith became part of something bigger. Later, Ruth gave birth to a son named Obed, and he became the grandfather of King David (Ruth 4:13–17). Jesus was born many years later through King David's family tree (Matthew 1:5–6, 16).

Why This Story Matters

Do we need any more proof that God lives in each one of us after reading Ruth's story? A Moabite woman goes to a foreign land without any prospects, family, or friends. She is motivated by the selfless goal of serving and supporting her mother-in-law. She doesn't know God, but she boldly tells Naomi: "Your God will be my God" (Ruth 1:16).

Ruth is the definition of faith in action.

She gave up everything and didn't think twice about it. She didn't hesitate or wonder how her life would work out. She simply followed her heart and moved to Bethlehem.

Ruth's story shows us that God sees us, even during our hardest moments. He saw the kindness of her heart and wove His great plan of salvation into her family legacy. Ruth had no idea that her story would change history. She loved first, and God did the rest.

A Prayer to End

Dear God, thank You for sharing Ruth's story with us and confirming what we already know: Everyone You create matters! Thank You for showing us what true faithfulness and service look like. Ruth's situation and life seemed hard and scary. How would she get food? Where would she sleep? Despite her challenges, she trusted in You wholly and completely, and You provided for her and Naomi. Teach us to trust Your plan. We know You always work for good, even when we can't see it. Amen.

Bible References

Ruth 1 — Ruth's loyalty to Naomi and return to Bethlehem
Ruth 2 — Ruth meets Boaz and gleans in his field
Ruth 4 — Boaz redeems Ruth, and they marry
Leviticus 19:9–10 — Law of gleaning for the poor
Deuteronomy 23:3–4 — Moabites excluded from the assembly
Matthew 1:5–6, 16 — Ruth in the genealogy of Jesus

~ 1050 Years Before Christ (BC)

Saul Anointed as King

Israel Asks for a King

As the period of the Judges came to an end, Israel warred with the Philistine nation and was losing the battle. The Israeli army retreated to its camp, devastated after losing thousands of men. Samuel the prophet, the leader of all of Israel, said to the people, "If you return to God, He will deliver you out of the hands of your enemy" (1 Samuel 7:3). On that day they agreed to serve the Lord with all their hearts, and He helped Israel route the Philistines (1 Samuel 7:10–13).

Samuel was highly respected by the entire population. For the rest of his life, he alone was the voice of Israel. As he neared the end of his life, Samuel appointed his sons, Joel and Abijah, to lead the people. But there was a problem with his decision: Samuel's sons were not fit to lead; they didn't have a heart for God (1 Samuel 8:1–3).

Israel's elders confronted Samuel and told him they didn't believe Joel and Abijah were the right ones to lead the people. They said to him, "Give us a king to lead us, just like all the other nations have!" (1 Samuel 8:5).

This news hurt Samuel. He knew that they really meant, "We don't want God to be our King anymore." So God told Samuel that He would give the people what they wanted, though He warned them that a human king wouldn't always be kind or fair. People make mistakes, even elected kings. But the people refused to listen to Samuel and said, "We want a king to lead us!" (1 Samuel 8:6–22).

A King That Looked the Part

In response, God appointed Saul, a man from the tribe of Benjamin, as king. He was a handsome man, taller than anyone else in Israel (1 Samuel 9:1–2). When people saw him, they said, "There is no one like him among the people" (1 Samuel 10:24).

Saul started off humble and insecure and couldn't believe God had selected him. "Why pick me?" he asked. "I'm from the smallest tribe in Israel. I'm a nobody" (1 Samuel 9:21). But God chose him for a reason, and at the proper time, God's Spirit came upon Saul, giving him the courage, confidence, and strength to lead (1 Samuel 10:6–7).

Saul performed his duties well for a while, and the nation of Israel supported him. He fought bravely against Israel's enemies, and the people prospered. But slowly, his attitude began to change.

A Heart Turns

Saul ruled Israel for forty-two years (1 Samuel 13:1), but he became proud and arrogant during his kingship. Instead of trusting in God, he began to make decisions out of fear, not faith.

For example, Samuel told Saul that he (Samuel) would offer a sacrifice before Saul's army went into battle to seek God's favor, acknowledging that victory ultimately depended on divine intervention, not the size of one's army. As the Philistine army closed in, Saul grew tired of waiting for Samuel. He rebelled against God's command and performed the sacrifice himself (1 Samuel 13:8–14).

Another time, Samuel instructed Saul to destroy everything within the nation of the Amalekites as punishment for their treatment of the Israelites when they left Egypt. Saul attacked the Amalekites, but instead of destroying everything, he imprisoned the king of the nation and took the Amalekites' treasure for himself and his army (1 Samuel 15:1–9).

Samuel asked Saul, "Why did you not follow through with what the Lord asked? I see King Agag here alive in front of me, along with his sheep, cows, and oxen." Saul said he kept the animals to provide a sacrifice to the Lord (1 Samuel 15:13–15).

Saul's response disappointed Samuel, who replied, "Does the Lord delight in burnt offerings and sacrifices as much as in obeying the Lord? To obey is better than sacrifice" (1 Samuel 15:22). Samuel continued, "Because you have rejected the word of the Lord, He has rejected you as king" (1 Samuel 15:23).

Samuel's announcement saddened Saul; he struggled to process the news. What king would take care of the Israelites if not him? But God already had an answer in someone unexpected. From the *outside*, people admired Saul's height; the next king, a young shepherd boy, was filled on the *inside* with a heart full of love for God (1 Samuel 16:1, 7).

Why This Story Matters

The Israelites wanted to imitate the other nations around them. They valued people, politics, kings, and armies more than their faith in God to take care of them. When they demanded a king, they chose someone who looked the part. Saul had the stature and appearance that seemed right in their eyes.

But God is not impressed by outward appearances. He looks at the heart. Are our hearts proud, jealous, and angry, or are they faithful, obedient, and trusting?

When our hearts are not in the right place, it is easy to drift off course, just like Saul did. In today's world, we are constantly tempted to choose what is popular over what is right. To become effective leaders and believers, we must be aligned with God from the inside out, ready to hear His voice and carry out His plans.

A Prayer to End

Dear God, teach us to seek You with humble hearts that truly desire to know who You are. As You shape our hearts, help us to build relationships that are rooted in love and understanding, seeing others for who they are on the inside, not just what we see on the surface. When we face difficult choices, give us the strength and wisdom to choose what is right, even when it's not easy. And when we fall short, give us the courage to come to You, to ask for forgiveness, and to grow so we don't repeat the same mistakes. Amen.

Bible References

1 Samuel 7 — Samuel urges Israel to return to the Lord
1 Samuel 8 — Israel demands a king
1 Samuel 9–10 — Saul is chosen and anointed
1 Samuel 13 — Saul disobeys by offering a sacrifice
1 Samuel 15 — Saul disobeys again; God rejects him
1 Samuel 16 — God chooses David as the next king

~ 1010 Years Before Christ (BC)

David — From Shepherd Boy to King of Israel

Humble Beginnings

David was the youngest of eight brothers from the family of Jesse. While his older brothers learned the art of war, David worked as a shepherd and spent his days in the fields caring for sheep, playing his harp, and speaking with God.

During this time, King Saul still ruled Israel but slowly started to turn away from the Lord. So God sent the prophet Samuel on a new mission to find Israel's next king in Bethlehem. The Lord said to Samuel, "Do not consider his appearance or his height, for the Lord does not look at the things people value, which are on the outside. I care about one's heart" (1 Samuel 16:7). Still, Samuel worried how he would accomplish this new task and keep it hidden from Saul. Saul's jealousy and unpredictable behavior were on the rise. If he learned God had chosen another king, he might kill the king and Samuel.

God told Samuel to take a cow with him on his journey, and if Saul asked, to tell him he was traveling to offer a sacrifice to the Lord (1 Samuel 16:2). Samuel went to the house of Jesse, who had eight sons. Once there, each boy presented himself to Samuel, from oldest to youngest. God reminded Samuel, "People look at the outside, but I look at the heart." In other words, God wouldn't select the new king based on age, strength, or height.

David was the last son presented, and while he stood in front of the prophet, the Lord's voice came to Samuel and said, "Rise and anoint him, this is the one" (1 Samuel 16:12). Samuel held a ceremony and anointed David with oil, marking him as God's chosen future king, although he wouldn't become king immediately (1 Samuel 16:13). After the ceremony, David went back to the same life he had before, working in the fields, caring for his sheep, and waiting for God's plan for his life to be revealed.

David and Goliath

While David waited, Israel warred with the Philistines. Each army occupied hills across from each other. Goliath, who served with the Philistine army, measured over nine feet tall and wore bronze armor that covered him from head to toe. At the height of the day, he glowed like the sun. For forty days, Goliath shouted at the army of Israel, daring someone to come out and fight him, but no one was brave enough (1 Samuel 17:16).

One day, David's father asked him to take food to his brothers who were on the front line of the battle. While there, David heard Goliath's challenge and was shocked that no one stood up to him. "Why isn't anyone standing up to him? Isn't there anyone in this army who trusts that God is bigger than this giant?" (1 Samuel 17:23–26).

King Saul received word that someone was willing to fight Goliath, so he summoned David to his tent. When David volunteered to fight the giant, Saul offered him his heavy armor, but David refused it. The gear didn't fit. David was not phased, and instead chose to fight Goliath with his sling, five smooth stones, and his faith (1 Samuel 17:32–40).

As David stood in front of the giant, Goliath laughed in disbelief that Israel had sent a boy to handle a man's job. The Philistine cursed David, but David confidently replied, "You come at me with a sword and spear, but I come at you in the name of the Lord" (1 Samuel 17:45).

As Goliath moved forward to attack, David sprinted out to meet him, slung a stone, and struck Goliath in the forehead. The giant fell forward face down to the ground and died (1 Samuel 17:48–50). Upon seeing this, Israel's army chased the Philistines and pushed back their army.

David became a hero that day and showed everyone that God was greater than any giant. He defeated Goliath not by his own strength but by the power of God.

Journey to Become King

King Saul invited David to serve him and gave him a high rank in the army. David became a great warrior who won many battles. Saul sensed that God was with David and grew jealous and fearful of his popularity, which grew daily among the people. An evil spirit tormented King Saul, and his fear eventually turned to rage. He tried to hurt David many times.

David spent years on the run (1 Samuel 18:6–12; 1 Samuel 19:1), but through it all, he trusted that God would protect him. He had many chances to fight back against Saul, but he never retaliated. Instead, he trusted God's promise that one day he'd be king and chose to patiently wait for God's timing (1 Samuel 24:1–7; 1 Samuel 26:8–11).

After Saul's death, King David ruled Israel with courage, kindness, and a heart that loved God deeply. He brought the Ark of the Covenant back to Jerusalem and turned the city into a beacon of hope (2 Samuel 6:12–15). David wasn't perfect, but each time he made a mistake, he always returned to God for forgiveness and guidance (Psalm 51).

Why This Story Matters

The Bible calls David "a man after God's own heart" because of his deep love and trust in the Lord (1 Samuel 13:14). David shows us that true courage and faith are not just about believing in God's plan, but waiting for the plan to unfold in God's way and His timing. That's the kind of faith David displayed on the front lines with his brothers when he volunteered to fight Goliath, fully confident that God would do something incredible through him on that battlefield.

This story reminds us that God created each of us for a purpose, no matter our age, size, or strength. There is no challenge too big for God. All we need to do is remain faithful, be patient, and trust that in His perfect timing, God will do something miraculous through our lives.

A Prayer to End

Dear God, thank You for sharing David's story with us. Help us to trust You as David did, so we can face our fears with courage. When others hurt us, teach us to forgive so our hearts aren't filled with revenge, jealousy, or anger. Remind us not to judge others by what we see on the outside, but to see them the way You do—by their hearts, by how they live, and by how they treat others. Give us patience and understanding, and help us remember that Your timing, though different from ours, is always perfect. Amen.

Bible References

1 Samuel 16 — Samuel anoints David
1 Samuel 17 — David defeats Goliath
1 Samuel 18–19 — Saul becomes jealous of David
1 Samuel 24, 26 — David spares Saul's life
2 Samuel 6 — David brings the Ark to Jerusalem
Psalm 51 — David's prayer for forgiveness
1 Samuel 13:14 — David called "a man after God's own heart"

~ 970 Years Before Christ (BC)

Solomon — The Wise King

A Humble Request

As King David's reign ended, the time came to select a new king to sit on the throne. God chose David's son, Solomon, to become the next ruler of Israel (1 Kings 1:28–30). But before Solomon became king, his father gave him important advice: "Be strong and always be obedient to God. Keep His laws and regulations as outlined by Moses." If Solomon followed his father's counsel, and his children and grandchildren also followed in God's ways, then a family member would always have a seat on the throne (1 Kings 2:1–4).

Solomon was about twenty years old when he heard these words and was probably overwhelmed by his appointment as the next king. After all, how could someone as young as him lead an entire nation? How would he rule people fairly? How would he learn to make wise decisions and keep everyone in the kingdom safe?

To calm his doubts, God spoke to him in a dream and said, "Ask me for whatever you want" (1 Kings 3:5). Although Solomon could have asked for money, power, fame, or victory over his enemies, he made a request that showed the intent of his heart:

"Lord, give me wisdom so I can be a good king and lead Your people well" (1 Kings 3:9).

God was so pleased with Solomon's humble request that He not only gave him more wisdom than anyone before or after him, but He also promised him riches, honor, and peace (1 Kings 3:10–14).

Greatest Wisdom

Solomon's gift of wisdom became famous across all the nations of the world. People traveled from faraway lands to hear him speak (1 Kings 4:29–34). He recited thousands of proverbs and sang thousands of songs by memory. If a visitor had a question about plant life, animals, or fish, Solomon told them about the biology behind their questions in a way they could understand.

When people could not resolve their quarrels, they brought them to Solomon. A well-known instance involved two women who came to him with one baby, though both claimed to be the child's mother (1 Kings 3:16–22). How could Solomon know who told the truth?

He considered what he heard from the women and then calmly asked for a sword and said, "Cut the baby in half and give each woman part of the child" (1 Kings 3:24–25).

The first woman shouted, "No! Please, give the baby to her. Don't kill him!" The other woman said, "Go ahead, cut him in two."

Then the king gave his ruling: "Give the baby to the first woman, she is his mother" (1 Kings 3:26–27). Solomon knew the woman who loved the baby enough to give him away must be the true mother. She received her child, and the onlookers were in awe of the king's wisdom.

Building the Temple

For the first time in decades, Israel wasn't at war with any neighboring country. This new-found peace gave Solomon the chance to do something his father David had always dreamed of: build a Temple for God (1 Kings 5:3–5).

Solomon made a treaty with Hiram, the King of Tyre, who was thrilled about the plans to build the Temple. Hiram agreed to supply Solomon all of the cedar wood, gold, and precious stones he needed to complete the project (1 Kings 5:6–10). Skilled craftsmen worked nonstop to ensure the Temple was the most beautiful building Israel had ever seen.

When the Temple of God was finally complete, Solomon placed the Ark of the Covenant into a special room he had built. He then prayed that God's presence would fill the Temple and that His Spirit would dwell among the people (1 Kings 8:6–13, 22–30).

Solomon's Big Mistake

Solomon ruled with wisdom and strength for most of his reign. That changed as he grew older and married foreign wives who worshiped false gods. He allowed those idols to enter the land, which caused the Israelites to go astray (1 Kings 11:1–8). The Lord became angry with Solomon; the wisest king sadly forgot that God alone is worthy of our worship and praise. Because of this, God allowed many foreign adversaries to rise up against him (1 Kings 11:9–14).

Why This Story Matters

Solomon began his reign over Israel with a heart that truly desired to follow God. He humbly sought God's guidance to address any weaknesses he had as a leader. God blessed Solomon's faithfulness, and his wisdom and success were known throughout the region. But as time passed, Solomon's priorities began to change. Between the riches he had gained and the appeal of foreign gods, Solomon slowly stopped seeking God's counsel and began to trust in his own wisdom.

When we ask God for help or guidance with a humble heart, we show that we need Him. But how do we react when the prayers are answered? If we take the credit and forget to thank God, we reveal pride in our hearts instead of gratitude. We must stay grounded and remember that every good thing comes from Him. In every high and low, may we always give God the glory He deserves.

A Prayer to End

Dear God, give us the wisdom to focus on the things that last forever and not on the temporary distractions of this world. Help us to recognize and use the unique gifts You've placed within each of us, gifts meant to honor You and not ourselves. Strengthen our faith so we can walk with You consistently, in both the good days and the bad ones. And as we trust You through every step, may our journey and personal story draw others closer to knowing who You are. Amen.

Bible References

1 Kings 1–2 — David appoints Solomon as king and gives his final advice
1 Kings 3 — Solomon asks for wisdom; a baby and two mothers
1 Kings 4 — Solomon's wisdom and knowledge
1 Kings 5–6 — Solomon prepares and builds the Temple
1 Kings 8 — Solomon dedicates the Temple
1 Kings 11 — Solomon's disobedience and downfall

~ 930 Years Before Christ (BC)

The Kingdom Divided —
Two Nations, Different Paths

A Simple Request

After King Solomon died, the once-united kingdom of Israel stood at a tipping point. Before his death, Solomon unfairly taxed and forced his people into slavery to ensure he would have enough resources to complete his palace and Temple building projects on time (1 Kings 11:27–28). When Solomon's son, Rehoboam, was next in line to rule, the people were concerned but hoped that the new king would show a little more kindness than his father.

The Israelite leaders gathered at a town called Shechem to crown Rehoboam as king. They had one simple request beforehand, though: "Please lighten the heavy burden your father placed on us. If you do, we will serve you faithfully" (1 Kings 12:3–4).

Rehoboam asked for a few days to consider their request. During that time, he sought advice from two groups. The first was an older group of men who had served his father wisely. They said, "If you serve the people kindly today, they will serve you forever" (1 Kings 12:6–7). He then asked a younger group of friends he grew up with for advice, and they gave a different response: "Be even tougher. Show them you are stronger than your father. Rule them with an iron fist" (1 Kings 12:8–11).

A Harsh Answer That Divides the Kingdom

Unfortunately, Rehoboam chose to follow the advice of the younger group and rule with pride and power. He spoke harshly to the people and said, "My father made the burden you carry heavy. I will make it even heavier. My father disciplined you with whips, but I will discipline you with scorpions" (1 Kings 12:14).

The people couldn't believe what they heard. Their hope for a gentle ruler vanished just like that. Feeling betrayed, they cried out, "What share do we have in David? We have no inheritance in the son of Jesse! To your tents, O Israel!" (1 Kings 12:16).

In that moment, everything in the kingdom changed. The ten tribes north of Israel decided to break away and create their own country. They rejected Rehoboam's reign and chose another man, Jeroboam, to lead them instead. Only the two southern tribes of Judah and Benjamin stayed to support Rehoboam and the house of David (1 Kings 12:19–20).

The great kingdom of Israel was split in two from that day forward. The northern kingdom kept the name Israel and was ruled by Jeroboam. Rehoboam ruled the southern kingdom, which was now called Judah.

It was a heartbreaking split, not just politically, but because neighbors who once lived side by side with their family tribes were now separated by borders. Brothers, sisters, cousins, and friends now found themselves living under the authority of different kings.

God Prevents a War

At first, Rehoboam thought about going to war with Israel to force the kingdom back together. He gathered an impressive army of 180,000 men to do battle against those in the northern kingdom (2 Chronicles 11:1), but God intervened and sent a prophet named Shemaiah with an important message: "Do not fight against your relatives. Go home, every man, for this thing is from Me" (1 Kings 12:22–24; 2 Chronicles 11:2–4). Remarkably, Rehoboam listened and called off the battle. The two kingdoms remained divided.

Israel Led into Idolatry

Jeroboam, the king of Israel, was concerned that his people, after traveling south to Jerusalem to worship in the Temple, would decide to stay in Judah and change their allegiance to King Rehoboam. To prevent this, Jeroboam made two golden calves and placed them in the cities of Bethel and Dan, so the people wouldn't have to leave Israel for worship services. He told the people, "Here are your gods, O Israel, who brought you out of Egypt!" (1 Kings 12:26–28).

He also built other areas called shrines where the people could pray and bring their sacrifices. The priests he appointed to work in these shrines were untrained and did not come from the tribe of Levi, as God commanded (1 Kings 12:31).

Even though the divided kingdoms seemed turned upside down, God's plan never failed. He made a promise to Jacob and David many years earlier that a forever King would come and bring peace to the world, ruling with perfect justice and mercy (2 Samuel 7:12–16). That promise was unfolding, even in the middle of so much brokenness.

Why This Story Matters

This story reminds us how quickly an entire nation can fall apart when leaders become prideful, surround themselves with foolish people, and make self-serving decisions. Over time, both Judah and Israel were ruled by twenty different kings each, most of whom continued to do evil in the eyes of the Lord and led their people to worship false gods. Despite repeated warnings, they refused to change.

The story is also a powerful reminder of the importance of living according to God's example: to love our neighbors as ourselves, to treat others and ourselves with respect, and to worship Him alone. When our hearts are transformed and we begin to live the life God wants us to live, we start to see glimpses of His Kingdom here on earth, just as it is in Heaven.

A Prayer to End

Dear God, when we are faced with big or small decisions in life, remind us to seek Your wisdom first. Surround us with family, friends, mentors, teachers, and coaches who will guide us in the right direction. Help us to lead by Your example, showing love, patience, and truth in all we do. May our choices reflect Your heart, and may our lives and our actions glorify You. Amen.

Bible References

2 Samuel 7: 12-16 — God establishes an eternal kingdom
1 Kings 11:26–43 — Solomon's sin and Jeroboam's rise
1 Kings 12:1–33 — Rehoboam's harsh decision and the division of the kingdom
2 Chronicles 10:1–19 — The people rebel against Rehoboam
2 Chronicles 11:1–4 — God's warning not to fight

DECEMBER 19

~ 740 Years Before Christ (BC)

Micah the Prophet — Speaks Justice and Hope

A Time of Corruption and Injustice

Long after Solomon's death, there was a dark period for hundreds of years when the Israelites no longer lived a godly life. Political leaders took advantage of their authority and became wealthy through theft and greed. They took property away from the rightful landowners illegally and used their influence to support the whims of the upper class. They were so focused on status and power that they no longer heard the cries of the poor (Micah 2:1–2; 3:1–3, 9–11).

The prophets were equally focused on personal financial gain. They were supposed to be the spiritual leaders of the community, ensuring all people were following the laws of the Torah, but they no longer spoke or sought truth. They blessed or turned a blind eye to injustices that were happening all over the region (Micah 3:5, 11).

Micah Stands in Truth

Micah lived in a small town called Moresheth, far away from major cities. He wasn't rich or powerful and didn't wear fancy clothes. One day, God came to him through a powerfully charged vision and showed him all that would happen to Israel and Judah if the people didn't change their evil ways. If they remained disobedient, the country of Assyria would come into Israel and destroy the city. Then the Babylonian army would come and destroy Judah, the Temple of God, and take its people away in exile (Micah 1:3–6; 3:12). Micah warned people throughout the region that it wasn't too late to change their ways, seek forgiveness, and live out God's plan, which was the light of the world to all nations (Micah 4:1–2).

God spoke to Micah, and Micah listened.

With a brave heart, Micah confronted Israel's leaders and citizens, saying the time had come for everyone to turn back to God. He said to the people, "God sees what's going on all over the region. He sees the lies, the greed, and the unfairness being shown to the people. And He cares. God wants His people to start living with kindness and turn away from evil things" (Micah 6:1–5).

Micah shared his message from the northern kingdom of Israel to the southern kingdom of Judah. He traveled tirelessly, day and night, all over the country, warning people to turn back to God. However, most of what he said fell on deaf ears.

The people Micah spoke to didn't want to hear the warnings. They were happy living their own way. In their minds, God wasn't their boss. Micah continued to speak to them anyway, hoping that some would listen.

Micah told the people exactly what God required of them, which had nothing to do with offering big sacrifices or hollow worship:

"What He really wants is for each person to do what is good, to act justly, to love mercy, and to walk humbly with your God" (Micah 6:8).

To some, Micah's words were offensive; they felt he judged them and tried to tell them how to live their lives. But he spoke honestly and from the heart, reminding them of the consequences they'd endure if they didn't change their ways. Though things seemed dark, Micah also tried to inspire the people by speaking about God's restoration for them all.

A Story of Hope and Love

Micah assured the people that despite the onslaught of foreign armies and dark times, God would never leave them or forget them. He promised to send a special person born out of the tribe of Judah to lead God's people with strength, justice, and kindness (Micah 5:2–4).

Micah prophesied about events that were 700 years into the future:

"But you, Bethlehem, though you are small among all the clans of Judah, out of you will come for Me one who will be ruler and King over all of Israel" (Micah 5:2). Bethlehem wasn't well known or powerful compared to other cities in the region, but God chose it as the birthplace for the future King of the world.

Micah may have lived a quiet life in a small town, but his message to Judah and Israel was huge. It was big enough to point all the way to our future Savior.

Why This Story Matters

Micah's story shows how a small-town man from humble beginnings was given a big message from God. He was called to speak the hard truth to people who didn't want to hear it, but he remained faithful and followed through with God's command because he trusted Him.

In life, it's often easier to "go with the flow," to blend in, or do what's popular instead of what's right. But let's be honest, evil forces in this world constantly work against God's truth and try to silence it. Micah didn't choose the easy road. He stood firm and stayed rooted in God's Word.

We are called to do the same, to be filled with His truth. When the time comes, God gives us the courage, the words, and the right moment to speak up for what is just and true. We can rest knowing that God's plans will never be denied and are always moving forward.

A Prayer to End

Dear God, thank You for giving us Micah's story as an example of what it means to stand firm in our faith, even in the face of great adversity, trusting that You are always with us. Give us hearts that desire to do what is right, even when no one else is watching. When You call us, give us the courage, voice, and words to make a difference in the lives of those around us. And give us the strength to stay focused on the plans You have put before us and not be distracted by the things of this world. Amen.

Bible References

Micah 1:1–6 — Warning of judgment over Israel and Judah
Micah 2–3 — Injustice by leaders and prophets
Micah 4 — A future kingdom of peace and restoration
Micah 5:2 — Prophecy of the Messiah born in Bethlehem
Micah 6:6–8 — What the Lord requires: justice, mercy, and humility

~ 725 – 585 Years Before Christ (BC)

Judah's Fall and Exile to Babylon

A Kingdom That Would Not Change

The Northern Kingdom of Israel fell after generations of disobedience, idolatry, and rejection of God's covenant promises to His people. Even though God sent many prophets with warnings to turn back to Him, including Elijah, Elisha, and Micah, the Israelites continued their wicked ways and ignored His commands. The kings of Israel did many evil things in the Lord's sight, leading the people further away from truth and justice. Eventually, God ran out of patience, and He brought His judgment upon them. In 722 BC, the Assyrian army invaded and took control of Israel. Many Israelites were captured and worked as slaves or scattered in fear to foreign lands, never returning to their homeland.

Despite the Assyrians being one step closer to Judah's border and the prophets' warnings coming true, Judah refused to change its ways.

Every now and then, a faithful king of Judah came to power and called the people back to God. For a while, the people made better choices, but over time, they turned back to their old habits and let evil consume them once again. They built false idols out of gold, silver, and bronze, and placed them in their homes. Some even brought them inside the Temple of God. They followed the religious practices of other nations, including offering their children as sacrifices. They were trapped in prideful living, choosing to go along with how everyone else lived rather than doing what was right and just.

Prophet after prophet came with warnings for them to repent of their sins: Isaiah, Jeremiah, Amos, Hosea, and Ezekiel. But hardly anyone listened.

God's Judgment Finally Arrives

Finally, God's patience wore thin. His love for the children of Israel gave way to discipline after their years of disobedience. Just as the prophets warned, judgment came. Babylon was used as God's instrument against Judah.

Babylon, led by the mighty King Nebuchadnezzar, swept across the land like a supernatural thunderstorm. The armies surrounded Jerusalem and cut off food and supplies. The people inside the city walls starved without clean water or bread. Battering rams destroyed the walls, exposing the city to its enemies. The people inside the city remembered the warnings of the prophets, but now, it was too late to fight back.

The Babylonian army attacked Jerusalem in waves over many years. The first time Babylon attacked, King Nebuchadnezzar took Judah's young leaders and nobles back with him as prisoners. Among the captives were teenagers Daniel, Hananiah, Mishael, and Azariah, who left their homes and lived in a foreign land (Daniel 1:1–7).

Still, Jerusalem stood a little longer.

The City and Temple Destroyed

Years later, Judah rebelled against Babylon by making an alliance with Egypt and refusing to pay the annual tribute. King Nebuchadnezzar responded with fury, destroying the entire city. He ordered that every home, every palace, and most painfully, the Temple of God be set on fire. The Temple, once filled with the glory of the Lord, was reduced to ashes (2 Kings 25:8–10).

As the city crumbled, Zedekiah, the king of Judah, tried to escape through a hole in the city wall at night. But the Babylonian army caught up with him. In one of the most heartbreaking scenes in the Bible, Zedekiah was forced to watch his sons get killed before his very eyes. Then the Babylonians took him back to Babylon in chains (2 Kings 25:6–7).

The survivors of the war were taken away, men, women, and children, and forced to walk hundreds of miles to Babylon. Their homes were destroyed, their city was gone, and they became strangers in a foreign land that did not worship the God of Israel.

Preparing for the Return

This period in history became known as the Babylonian Exile, just as God had shared through the prophet Jeremiah:

"This whole country will become a desolate wasteland, and these nations will serve the king of Babylon seventy years" (Jeremiah 25:11).

During their exile, God kept His promises. Even though the Temple fell, and the city was in ruins, God was still working. He prepared His people for a return, a rebuilding, and a future King who would one day restore everything they lost.

Why This Story Matters

The story of Judah's exile to Babylon is a powerful reminder that we have a gracious and patient God. He gave the leaders of Judah and Israel many chances to turn back to Him, sending prophet after prophet to warn them of what would happen if they continued down the wrong path. But they refused to listen, and in time, both nations were conquered.

As we go out into the world, we need to stay alert to God's voice, through the quiet prompting in our hearts and the people He places around us. The more we draw close to Him, the more clearly we'll recognize when He is leading us. This story of exile is a strong reminder to listen for God's voice early and to take His warnings seriously.

A Prayer to End

Dear God, thank You that even when we stray from Your path, You are never far away. Thank You for Your loving correction that brings us back to You. Help us to listen closely and recognize the sound of Your voice so we don't confuse it with our own, especially when making big decisions. Thank You for Your grace and mercy, which we don't deserve but that You give so freely. Amen.

Bible References

2 Kings 24–25 — Fall of Jerusalem and destruction of the Temple
Jeremiah 25:1–14 — Prophecy of seventy years in exile
Daniel 1 — Daniel and friends taken into exile

~ 605 – 530 Years Before Christ (BC)

Daniel Blessed in Babylon

When the people of Judah were taken into exile, some of the most talented young men were chosen by the king of Babylon to serve in his palace. Daniel was one of them. Along with his friends, Shadrach, Meshach, and Abednego, they were taught a new language and educated in Babylonian history. The exiles were trained so that they would forget their old lives, their God, and their religious traditions. However, Daniel and his friends decided that no matter what they were taught, they would never turn their backs on their God (Daniel 1:1–4).

Every day, a certain group of men of Judah had the opportunity to eat food and drink wine from King Nebuchadnezzar's table. Daniel knew that the current Jewish law forbade eating many foods available at the king's table, so he politely asked for permission to eat only vegetables and drink water. The palace officials were concerned that if they accepted Daniel's request, the king might notice that he and his friends looked weaker than the others. But Daniel suggested that they be allowed to eat their simple diet for a period of ten days, and then they could see which group looked healthier (Daniel 1:5, 8–14).

After just a few days, Daniel and his friends looked a lot healthier and stronger than anyone else. God honored their obedience. Their continued faith not only helped them grow physically stronger, but God also gave them knowledge, wisdom, and understanding far beyond all others in Babylon (Daniel 1:15–17).

Ability to Interpret Dreams

As time passed, King Nebuchadnezzar began to have troubling dreams. None of his magicians or wise men could explain them, but Daniel turned to God to seek His counsel. God revealed the meaning of the king's dream to Daniel during the night. When Daniel explained what his dream meant, the king was so amazed that he praised the God of Daniel and placed him in a position of great honor (Daniel 2:1–11, 18-19, 24–49). It was clear to everyone that Daniel's wisdom came from a higher source … not from Babylon, but from the God of Israel.

Faithful in the Fire

One day, King Nebuchadnezzar built a huge golden statue that measured ninety feet tall. Out in the courtyard of his palace, he demanded that everyone bow down and worship it.

Trumpets played loudly across the city, and whenever the music played, every person was expected to bow down on the ground before the statue (Daniel 3:1, 4–5). Shadrach, Meshach, and Abednego refused to do so. They only bowed down to the one true God (Daniel 3:12).

The king got angry when he heard about their disobedience. He gave them one more chance to bow down and threatened to throw them into a fiery furnace if they refused. They answered courageously, "If we are thrown into the blazing furnace, the God we serve is able to deliver us from it. But even if He does not, we want you to know, O king, that we will not serve your gods" (Daniel 3:13–18).

Nebuchadnezzar's rage burned. He ordered that the furnace fire be turned up seven times hotter, and he commanded the three young men to be thrown into the fire together. The furnace was so hot that the soldiers who threw them in immediately died from the heat (Daniel 3:19–23).

Then, something miraculous happened. Once Shadrach, Meshach, and Abednego were tossed into the fire, Nebuchadnezzar saw something he couldn't explain. "Weren't there three men we tied up and threw into the fire?" he asked. "Look! I see four men walking around in the fire, unbound and unharmed, and the fourth looks like a son of the gods!" (Daniel 3:24–25).

Many people believe that Jesus stood in the furnace with them, rescuing them from the flames. When they came out of the pit, not one single hair on their heads was burned. Nebuchadnezzar couldn't believe it. He was in awe of what he had witnessed and praised the God of Shadrach, Meshach, and Abednego. He ordered that no one could speak against the God of Israel (Daniel 3:28–29).

Jealousy and Redemption in the Lion's Den

After some time, a king named Darius came to power in Babylon. Daniel continued to rise in position because of his honesty, wisdom, and leadership; other officials became jealous and plotted against him. They tricked King Darius into making this law: For thirty days, no one other than the king could pray, and if anyone broke this rule, they would be put to death (Daniel 6:1–9).

Daniel heard about the law but remained faithful to God and continued to pray to Him three times a day. The next morning, while he prayed in his room, the envious officials barged in and caught him. They took Daniel straight to the king (Daniel 6:10–11).

Daniel broke the king's edict and was sentenced to death. His punishment? He was to be thrown into a lion's den. King Darius tried to stop this ruling, but by law, a king's decree could not be broken. So, the king reluctantly gave the order, and Daniel was tossed into the den with a group of ferocious lions. But God sent an angel to close their mouths, and Daniel remained safe with the lions all night (Daniel 6:14–16, 22).

The next morning, King Darius hurried to the lion's den and cried out, "Daniel, servant of the living God, has your God been able to rescue you?" To his delight, Daniel answered that he was alive and that his God had protected him (Daniel 6:19–22).

After this, King Darius issued a decree: All people must honor Daniel's God, the God of Israel. The king highly esteemed Daniel, who lived and served faithfully, and even received visions from God about future kingdoms (Daniel 6:25–28).

Why This Story Matters

Daniel's life reminds us that no matter where we are or what our situation may be, we are called to live with courage, faith, and unwavering trust in God. Daniel, Shadrach, Meshach, and Abednego chose faith over fear and obedience over compromise. These friends understood that their loyalty to God mattered more than the opinions or threats of men.

We can rest assured that God will show up in powerful and unexpected ways to support and protect us in our time of need. What He asks of us is the courage to stand firm in our faith, whether we're facing a fire or standing inside a lion's den. No matter what, God will always be by our side.

A Prayer to End

Dear God, thank You for the strength You gave Daniel, Shadrach, Meshach, and Abednego to make the right choices in the face of great adversity. Help us to be courageous and stand up for You, even when it is hard or when we feel alone. Give us hearts that trust You fully and completely, no matter what challenges we face. And help us be bold in our faith, sharing who You are with those around us. Amen.

Bible References

Daniel 1:1–21 — Daniel and friends chosen and tested
Daniel 2:1–49 — Daniel interprets Nebuchadnezzar's dream
Daniel 3:1–30 — The fiery furnace: Shadrach, Meshach, and Abednego
Daniel 6:1–28 — Daniel in the lion's den

~ 540 – 515 Years Before Christ (BC)

The Return from Exile and Rebuilding the Temple

The Long-Awaited Return

For seventy years, God's people lived in Babylon, in exile, far away from the land He had promised the descendants of Abraham, Isaac, and Jacob. A number of Jewish people lived in Babylon most of their lives with families that were born in exile and had never seen Jerusalem. The folk songs of Zion became whispers in a foreign land, and the once-great Temple of God was just a memory.

Yet, God never forgot His promises. Through the prophet Jeremiah, God announced that He would bring His people back home after seventy years (Jeremiah 29:10). Even when everything seemed lost, His word and His promises stood the test of time.

When a new king came to power, King Cyrus of Persia, something amazing happened. Unlike the Babylonian kings who came before him, King Cyrus had a different spirit. One night, God changed his heart, and King Cyrus issued a decree that allowed the people of Judah to return to Jerusalem. The decree also ordered the returning Israelites to rebuild the Temple of the Lord. King Cyrus encouraged anyone who wished to leave to also take part in this great mission (Ezra 1:1–4).

Imagine the excitement that came with that news! After seventy years in exile, families were allowed to return home. Elders who still remembered and longed for Jerusalem probably wiped tears from their eyes. Fifty thousand people set out for a long journey home, with God's blessing and Cyrus' order. King Cyrus also gave them back the precious silver and gold Temple items that Nebuchadnezzar had looted years before (Ezra 1:5–7).

Worship Restored

The people returned to a city that was in complete ruins, led by a man named Zerubbabel and a priest named Jeshua. Jerusalem's walls had collapsed, the once-glorious Temple was nothing but rubble, and the town was eerily deserted.

But the people did not lose heart. The very first thing they did was rebuild the altar out of a love for God. Even before they started to rebuild the Temple itself, they needed a place to worship and offer sacrifices to God. They rebuilt the altar on its original foundation by placing stones with great care and offered burnt offerings morning and night, just as God commanded (Ezra 3:1–6). These offerings represented the people seeking forgiveness for their sins, their devotion to God, and their gratitude for their blessings.

Then they started work on the foundation for the new Temple. The people held a great celebration when it was completed. Trumpets and harps sounded. Cymbals crashed. The Levite priests worshiped God, saying, "For He is good, for His steadfast love endures forever toward Israel!" (Ezra 3:11).

But not everyone was excited about the project. Some of the older men and women wept uncontrollably, remembering what Solomon's Temple looked like in its splendor. They knew from the new foundation that the rebuilt Temple would never match the size, the beauty, or the glory of what the Temple was before (Ezra 3:12).

Encouraged and Strengthened by the Spirit

Soon, trouble came to Jerusalem. Enemies living in nearby towns tried to stop the rebuilding of the city. They harassed and made fun of the Israelites while they worked. They even sent letters filled with lies to kings and officials in foreign lands, warning them to be concerned about the city's rebirth and trying to convince them to step in, interfere, and slow down the people's progress (Ezra 4:1-24).

God sent words of encouragement through two prophets, Haggai and Zechariah, to keep everyone focused on the task at hand. They told them, "Be strong … for I am with you, declares the Lord" (Haggai 2:4). And "Not by might, nor by power, but by My Spirit"; rebuilding the Temple would only happen by God's Spirit and not by human intervention (Zechariah 4:6).

The people picked up their tools once again and continued their work, encouraged and energized by God's promises. Despite facing daily obstacles, they rebuilt the Temple with determination and faith. As they approached the completion, their hearts overflowed with happiness, joy, and peace as they saw God's glory return to Jerusalem.

The Israelites were back in their land. The Temple was rebuilt. Worship was restored (Ezra 6:13–22). But things still weren't like they used to be. They were still under the rule of foreign kings. Their hearts longed for the true King, the One the prophets had promised, the Messiah.

Then, the waiting began. For the next four hundred years, no more prophets spoke and no new words came from God. It was a time of silence, a time of waiting.

But God had not forgotten His promise. His greatest promise was about to come true. The Savior was on His way.

Why This Story Matters

When God allowed the Israelites to return to Jerusalem after seventy years, they immediately built an altar and gave thanks to Him. Day and night, they worshiped and praised God. They recognized that their long-awaited prayers had finally been answered, and their freedom restored.

Do we respond the same way when good things happen in our own lives? Do we pause to thank God and give Him the glory, or do we get caught up in the celebration and forget the One who made it all possible? Worship should always remain at the center of our lives. When we follow God and live out the life He intends for us, we experience true peace that guides us with purpose and love.

As the Israelites began the Lord's work in rebuilding the Temple in Jerusalem, opposition quickly arose — evil revealed itself in an attempt to halt the progress. The same is true today: When we step into God's calling, speak His truth, and share His Word, we can expect resistance from the forces of darkness that seek to hinder us from being the salt and light of the world. To stand firm, we must clothe ourselves with the Spirit of God, trusting that in every battle, we are never alone.

A Prayer to End

Dear God, thank You for being a God of new beginnings. When life feels out of control and hope begins to fade away, help us remember that You are always at work, even when we can't see it. Teach us to be patient and trust Your perfect timing. Strengthen us to feel Your presence when we speak Your truth, and shield us from the darkness that tries to pull us away. When it feels like the world is falling apart, give us the wisdom, energy, and words we need to keep advancing Your Kingdom. Amen.

Bible References

Jeremiah 29:10 — A promise of rescue after seventy years in exile
Ezra 1:1–11 — The decree of Cyrus and the return home
Ezra 3:1–13 — Rebuilding the altar and laying the Temple foundation
Ezra 4:1–24 — Opposition to the work
Haggai 1–2 — Encouragement to rebuild the Temple
Zechariah 4:6 — Divine power is greater than our limitations
Ezra 6:13–22 — Completion and celebration of the Temple

DECEMBER 23

~ 1 Year Before Christ (BC)

The Angel's Message of a Future King

For hundreds of years, God's people waited. They remembered prophets' words that had come before them. They spoke of a promise long ago … that a Savior would come, a special person sent by God to rescue the world from sin and darkness. But for a long period of time, there was only silence.

Then, on a clear, quiet night in Nazareth — a small town of Galilee — God sent an angel to a young woman named Mary (Luke 1:26–27). She was a simple girl of strong faith engaged to Joseph, a man of great character. Their lives were about to take a miraculous, unexpected turn.

Mary Receives Miraculous News

As Mary went about her day, she noticed that the air around her seemed to change. Suddenly, the angel Gabriel appeared in front of her, his voice full of kindness and authority.

"Greetings, Mary. You are highly favored. The Lord is with you." Mary was greatly troubled at his words and wondered, "What kind of greeting was this?" (Luke 1:28–29).

But Gabriel shared words that changed history:

"Do not be afraid, Mary. You have found favor with God. You will give birth to a son, and you are to name Him Jesus. He will be great and will be called the Son of the Most High. His kingdom will never end" (Luke 1:30–33).

Mary asked, "How will this happen? I am not even married" (Luke 1:34).

Gabriel explained, "The Holy Spirit will come upon you, and the child born to you will be holy, the very Son of God" (Luke 1:35).

Mary remained faithful to God and responded, "I am the Lord's servant. May it be to me just as you have said" (Luke 1:38).

Joseph Encouraged

Mary wasn't the only one who needed strong faith and courage to carry out Gabriel's message.

Joseph wasn't sure how to respond when Mary first told him she was pregnant. He knew they had not consummated their union, so Joseph knew the child couldn't be his.

His heart must have ached as he considered his next steps. Should he stay with Mary or leave her? Joseph was a good man who didn't want to hurt Mary's feelings. At one point, he thought his best course of action was to walk away quietly. One thing he knew for sure: Whatever he decided would embarrass and shame both families (Matthew 1:19).

Later that night, the angel Gabriel appeared to Joseph in a dream. "Joseph, son of David," the angel said, "do not be afraid to take Mary as your wife. Because what is conceived in her is from the Holy Spirit. She will give birth to a son, and you are to name Him Jesus, because he will save His people from their sins" (Matthew 1:20–21).

When Joseph woke up, the heavy burden he had carried was gone. He was filled with an indescribable peace in his heart. His faith was strong, and he believed the words Gabriel spoke to him. Joseph chose to obey God, to stand by Mary's side, and to raise the Son of God as his own.

The Greatest Promise Put into Motion

And so, the greatest story in the world began, not in a castle, not with a fireworks display, but with two ordinary people who had great faith. God chose Mary and Joseph because of their courage and willingness to say "Yes" to His plan.

Mary was with child, and Joseph stood by her side. They trusted that God was unfolding a plan greater than either of them could imagine.

Soon, the Savior, King Jesus, would enter the world, born in the unlikeliest of places.

Why This Story Matters

The story of Mary and Joseph shows us that God can use ordinary people to do extraordinary things. He chooses people to carry out His plans based on their love for Him and their faithful hearts, not according to their wealth, popularity, or strength.

God pulled Joseph and Mary out of the lives they knew and were accustomed to. They followed God's plan because of their great belief in Him. Mary's mission seemed like an impossible task, but she said, "Yes." Joseph knew he'd face ridicule by supporting Mary, but when asked to stay, he said, "Yes." Mary and Joseph trusted God completely. Even though they couldn't comprehend how His plan would unfold, they both were willing to be part of it.

Thanks to their obedience, Jesus would enter our broken world to bring hope, salvation, and love to people and nations all over the world.

A Prayer to End

Dear God, thank You for sharing the amazing story of Mary and Joseph. Help us learn to have the faith they had, so that when we are called, even if things get tough, we will be brave enough to say, "Yes." May our lives reflect Your Spirit so clearly that those who don't yet know You are drawn in with curiosity, eager to ask and learn more about who You are. Amen.

Bible References

Luke 1:26–38 — The angel Gabriel appears to Mary and announces the birth of Jesus

Matthew 1:18–25 — An angel appears to Joseph in a dream, telling him to take Mary as his wife and explaining Jesus' birth

DECEMBER 24

~ 1 Year Before Christ (BC)

The Way for Jesus Begins

A Surprise Message — Zechariah and Elizabeth's Miracle

Before Jesus was born, God prepared the way for Him to come into the world, just as the prophets had promised. They told of someone who would come first, a strong voice of truth crying out from the wilderness, calling the people to get ready for the arrival of a great Savior. More than seven hundred years earlier, the prophet Isaiah spoke about this moment: "A voice of one calling: 'In the wilderness prepare the way for the Lord; make straight in the desert a highway for our God'" (Isaiah 40:3). Isaiah spoke of John the Baptist, whose own story began with a miracle.

Zechariah was a faithful priest from the tribe of the Levites. He and his wife, Elizabeth, both loved the Lord deeply, but they still faced loss in their lives. They couldn't have children. For many years, they went to God and prayed for a child, but now that they were old, pregnancy seemed impossible (Luke 1:5–7).

Zechariah performed priestly duties within the Temple throughout the year. One day, as he burned incense, which was a pleasing aroma to God, the angel Gabriel appeared beside the altar (Luke 1:8–11).

"Do not be afraid, Zechariah," Gabriel said. "Your prayer has been heard. Elizabeth will have a son, and you will name him John. He will prepare the people for the coming of the Savior" (Luke 1:13).

Zechariah was shocked. "How can this be? We are too old," he whispered (Luke 1:18).

Because he did not believe the angel's words, Gabriel shut Zechariah's mouth so he could not speak until the child was born. Can you imagine how Zechariah felt? He waited his whole life for a child, and now, after hearing the joyful news that his wife would get pregnant, he couldn't share his excitement with anyone (Luke 1:20–23).

Elizabeth eventually became pregnant, and their once quiet home was suddenly filled with excitement, hope, and wonder.

A Joyful Reunion — Mary Visits Elizabeth

When the angel Gabriel visited Mary (discussed in the December 23 passage), he told her of her relative Elizabeth's pregnancy. Mary's heart was full of happiness upon hearing the news, and she went to visit Elizabeth in the hill country of Judea.

The moment Mary arrived and called out to Elizabeth, Elizabeth felt the baby leap inside her womb. Filled with the Holy Spirit, she cried out joyfully, "Blessed are you, Mary, and blessed is the child you carry!" (Luke 1:42).

Even before Elizabeth's son was born, he felt Jesus' presence and leaped for joy. That unborn child eventually became known as John the Baptist. What a beautiful moment between these two women, both chosen by God to mother two special children. They shared in the wonder of God's promises coming to pass.

Caesar's Census — The Plan Unfolds

Meanwhile, far away, the leader of the Roman Empire, Caesar Augustus, issued an order. "Everyone must return to their family's hometown to be counted for a census so Caesar knows the total number of people living under his rule" (Luke 2:1–5)

For Caesar, maintaining his military power and control over the known world cost a lot of money. So, he needed to ensure each person paid him a tax to further expand his empire. What Caesar didn't know was that the census order required all people to return to their hometowns and be counted. God was using this moment to fulfill a promise He had made long ago — that the Savior would be born in Bethlehem (Micah 5:2).

Back in Nazareth, the time was drawing near for Mary to deliver her child. Joseph, who cared for her, heard about Caesar's order and knew he and Mary needed to travel nearly ninety miles to his family's hometown, Bethlehem.

The journey was hard, especially for pregnant Mary, who sat atop a rambling donkey. Joseph walked alongside Mary, guiding them through rugged hills and hot, dusty plains. Mile by mile, they moved closer to their fateful destination, and God was with them every step of the way.

Why This Story Matters

This story reminds us that God is always at work behind the scenes for good. He heard the prayers of Zechariah and Elizabeth and answered them in a miraculous way, giving them a child even in their old age. He used the Roman emperor's census, a decision made by someone who didn't believe in God, to set His greater plan into motion. Mary and Joseph arrived in Bethlehem at just the right time because of Caesar's order. Their travels to the land fulfilled the prophecy that the Savior would be born there. Every step was guided by God, showing that His plan is always unfolding, even through unexpected events.

We can take comfort knowing that the same God is still at work in our lives today. Even when we don't fully understand, He is guiding our steps, answering prayers, and weaving together His perfect plan. Just like in the days of Mary and Joseph, God is in control of all the details. His timing is never late. And when we trust in Him, we can be sure that He is leading us exactly where we need to be.

A Prayer to End

Dear God, thank You for reminding us that even when life feels ordinary, You are still at work, carrying out Your perfect plan. Help us to trust You, even when You call us to do what feels impossible or when the way that lies ahead is difficult. Open our eyes to see the road You have set before us, and guide us as we walk the straight and narrow path that leads to the salvation only found through You. Amen.

Bible References

Isaiah 40:3 — Prepare the way for the Lord
Luke 1:5–25 — The angel Gabriel appears to Zechariah
Luke 1:39–56 — Mary visits Elizabeth
Luke 2:1–7 — The census and Mary and Joseph's journey to Bethlehem
Micah 5:2 — Prophecy of the Savior's birth in Bethlehem

DECEMBER 25

In the Year of Our Lord 1 (AD)

Jesus is Born!

The Road to Bethlehem

Mary and Joseph approached the small, sleepy town of their ancestors. This was the same town the prophets spoke of throughout the Bible, the place where a future King would be born, and the very place where King David had come from — Bethlehem (1 Samuel 16:1; Luke 2:4).

The prophet Micah proclaimed, "Bethlehem, though you are small among all the tribes, from you will come the ruler over all of Israel" (Micah 5:2). This once-quiet town was now bustling with people because of Caesar's census decree. The local inns were filled with guests who had traveled from regions far and wide.

The appointed time had come. The baby that the angel of God had promised was ready to be born (Luke 1:30–33).

Joseph hoped to find a warm and safe place for them to stay, but no rooms were available. Finally, one innkeeper offered a place; not a warm guest room, but a simple, lowly stable used to house animals that belonged to guests who stayed at the inn that night.

Salvation Found in a Manger

No attendants were present to help Mary deliver her child. Only Joseph was there, and the blessings God bestowed upon them. In that moment, without any fanfare and surrounded by the sounds of animals and the smell of hay, Mary gave birth to the Son of God. Jesus, the Savior of the world, had arrived (Luke 2:6–7).

Mary lovingly wrapped her baby in cloths and laid Him gently in a manger, a feeding trough filled with straw, and quietly admired Him while He slept. King Jesus had come into the world in the most humble and unassuming way.

The Angel's Message to the Shepherds

Not far from Bethlehem was a group of shepherds who kept watch over their flocks. They were ordinary men who worked long, cold nights under the stars to ensure their animals stayed safe (Luke 2:8).

This particular night started like any other but ended up being one unlike any they had ever seen. A brilliant light appeared around them, and out of the light came an angel of the Lord. The shepherds quaked with fear (Luke 2:9).

The angel said, "Do not be afraid. I bring you good news of great joy that will be for all people. Today, in the town of David, a Savior has been born to you; He is Christ the Lord" (Luke 2:10–11).

The angel's words pierced their hearts and filled the shepherds with hope and peace.

"This will be a sign to you: You will find a baby wrapped in cloths and lying in a manger" (Luke 2:12).

Then, the heavens exploded with light. A group of angels appeared and sang, "Glory to God in the highest, and on earth peace to those on whom His favor rests!" (Luke 2:13–14).

The Shepherds' Journey to See the Messiah

As quickly as the angels appeared, they were gone. Once again, the night was silent. The shepherds looked at each other, their hearts pounding, unable to fully comprehend what they'd just seen. With excitement, they said, "Let's go to Bethlehem! Let's see this thing that has happened, which the Lord has told us about!" (Luke 2:15).

They hurried out, and once they arrived in Bethlehem, they searched until they found the stable (Luke 2:16).

Once there, in the quiet of the night, they entered the stable and found Mary and Joseph looking down at a baby wrapped in warm cloth. The shepherds approached Jesus and knelt, their eyes tearing up and wide open with wonder. They were the first ones to see the promised newborn King, the Savior who came into a world that desperately needed Him (Luke 2:16).

Sharing the Good News

The shepherds left the presence of the living God, ran through the streets, and loudly proclaimed to the people in Bethlehem what they had heard and seen. Everyone who listened to their story was amazed (Luke 2:17–18).

The shepherds returned to care for their flock, glorifying and praising God for all they had witnessed. Their hearts were forever changed the night they met the Savior King (Luke 2:20).

Why This Story Matters

Mary and Joseph arrived in Bethlehem to find the town crowded and full. They didn't receive a special welcome, and there was no place prepared for them to stay. But God was not absent. He provided shelter in the most unexpected way: a quiet, humble stable. The location wasn't lavish, but it was exactly enough. Enough space. Enough warmth. Enough peace for a King to be born.

The birth of Jesus reminds us that God never forgets His promises. He always shows up, even if it's not in the way we expect. His provision often comes quietly, through simple, ordinary moments. Mary and Joseph weren't given riches, but they had God's protection, peace, and presence, and that was more than enough.

God's love didn't come through royal fanfare or palace gates, but through the cries of a baby in a manger. Jesus came not as a ruler demanding loyalty, but as a servant offering hope and grace to help reconcile the world back to God.

A Prayer to End

Dear God, thank You for loving us enough to see that we could never reconcile ourselves back to You. Because of that great love, You sent Your Son, Jesus, so we could know You more deeply. The gift You gave so freely, though we didn't deserve it, is the perfect Christmas gift. Help us remember that Your mercy and grace are for everyone, and that Your love reaches the rich and the poor, the powerful and the weak, the believer and those who have yet to discover who You are. For all our days, may our hope and peace be found in You. Amen.

Bible References

1 Samuel 16:1 — Bethlehem is identified as the hometown of King David

Micah 5:2 — Prophecy that a ruler of Israel would come from Bethlehem

Luke 1:30–33 — The angel Gabriel tells Mary she will give birth to the Son of God

Luke 2:1–7 — Caesar's census leads Mary and Joseph to Bethlehem, where Jesus is born and laid in a manger

Luke 2:8-20 — God chooses the humble to reveal His glory

In the Year of Our Lord 1 (AD)

The Journey of the Wise Men

Ancient Prophecies and a Hopeful Promise

Far to the east — beyond the valleys and rivers, desert plains and mountains — lived a group of wise men, called Magi. These men were scholars who spent their lives studying nature's living things, reading the stars, and learning about ancient prophecies. They weren't royalty, but they were important, highly respected men known for their great knowledge and wisdom.

One quiet night, as they searched the sky, a star brighter and more magnificent than any they had ever seen before appeared. They came together to discuss what they saw and recounted the ancient words of the prophets that spoke of a future King sent by God, a Savior who would rule the world with justice and peace.

The prophecy said, "A star will come out of Jacob; a scepter will rise out of Israel," (Numbers 24:17).

The Magi packed their belongings, gathered gifts of gold, frankincense, and myrrh — treasures fit for a king — and began the long journey. The special star they saw guided them on their journey westward. They weren't sure where they were headed or how long it would take to get there, but they knew the opportunity to see the King would be worth it.

Meeting with King Herod

The Magi entered Jerusalem and requested a meeting with the Roman-appointed leader, King Herod of Judea. He was a distrustful, jealous leader who constantly feared that those he ruled were working to unseat him. Therefore, he ruled the land with a heavy hand, oppressing the people with hard labor and heavy taxes.

When they stood before Herod, the Magi asked, "Where is the one who has been born king of the Jews? We saw his star when it rose and have come to worship him" (Matthew 2:2).

King Herod was very disturbed when he heard them speak in this way (Matthew 2:3). He called his royal priests and teachers together and inquired of them where the Messiah had been born. They told him the prophets' prediction: that a ruler, a king, would be born in Bethlehem (Matthew 2:4–5).

Herod met secretly with the Magi to find out what they knew, specifically, when they first saw this wonderful star that guided them. He requested that once the child was found, they hurry back to his palace and let him know the location of the child so he, too, could come and worship Him. After hearing this, the Magi left King Herod and went on their way (Matthew 2:7-9).

A Faithful Journey

The Magi's travel was difficult. They pressed on through dusty, cold nights and endless miles, but they kept their eyes on the shining star that guided them. Day after day, they traveled faithfully, one step closer to their destination.

As they approached Bethlehem, their hearts were full of excitement. They were mesmerized by the thought of meeting the one true King who was sent to change the world.

Gifts for a King

When the Magi saw the star stop and rest over a stable, they were overwhelmed with joy. They unpacked their gifts and slowly entered the stable. "There they saw the child in Mary's arms and immediately bowed down on their knees and worshiped him" (Matthew 2:11).

The Magi prayed over the gifts of gold, frankincense, and myrrh that they set before King Jesus. They hoped the gifts would be received with the same love they were gifted (Matthew 2:11).

After they spent the night in Bethlehem, they were warned in a dream not to return to Herod or to disclose Jesus' location. So, they returned home a different way (Matthew 2:12).

The Magi were not Jewish and didn't fully understand everything that had occurred, but their hearts were open, and they trusted in God's plan. Little did they know that Jesus had come not for one nation, but for the entire world.

Why This Story Matters

This story is a beautiful reminder that those of us who truly seek God will find Him. No matter where we come from, how far we have to go, or how long the journey takes, God's guiding light is available to all who are willing to follow Him.

The Magi weren't part of God's chosen people, yet through Jesus, they became part of His promised family, forever.

They also weren't afraid to speak the truth. The Bible says that when they told Herod why they were there, their announcement disturbed him and "all" of Jerusalem. The Magi showed great bravery when they let the current appointed king know that they searched for the "King of the Jews." They demonstrated abundant faith in God by leaving behind what was comfortable and trusting that God would lead them every step of the way.

A Prayer to End

Dear God, thank You for the example of the Magi, who were prepared for the task set before them. Help us to be like them, open and willing to follow wherever You lead, no matter how difficult the journey may be. Teach us to learn from Your Word, to walk in Your ways, and to stand firmly on Your truth. Give us the confidence to go out into the world and boldly share Your story with others, in our communities and across the globe. Amen.

Bible References

Numbers 24:17 — God reveals hope found in Jesus

Matthew 2:1–12 — The wise men see the star, travel to Jerusalem, and visit Jesus, bringing gifts

Simeon and Anna Worship the Future King; Mary and Joseph Escape to Egypt

After Jesus Was Born

Mary and Joseph knew they were part of a miraculous plan. But they also knew they needed to follow the laws of the land. So, they departed Bethlehem and made the long, difficult journey back to Jerusalem, where they would follow religious tradition and present Jesus to God in the Temple.

Simeon Waits for a Promise

There was a man named Simeon in Jerusalem, a righteous and honest man who loved God with all his heart. God promised him that he would not die until he had seen the Messiah, baby Jesus, with his own eyes. Simeon waited patiently for the arrival of the future King. Day after day, he walked to the Temple, watching, waiting, and praying for the Messiah to arrive. Even though time passed and he grew old, Simeon never stopped believing that God's promise would come to pass (Luke 2:25–26).

One day, because the Spirit of God was with Simeon, he heard a whisper encouraging him, "Today, go down to the Temple. Today is the day" (Luke 2:27).

Simeon Praises Jesus

As Mary carried her baby into the Temple courts, Simeon's eyes lit up. He knew instantly that this child was the One he had been waiting to see his entire life. With trembling hands and tears of happiness welling up in his eyes, Simeon took baby Jesus and lifted Him high in the air with both hands, praising God for blessing mankind with this life-changing gift (Luke 2:28).

Simeon continued to praise God and said, "Sovereign Lord, now You can let Your servant die in peace, just as You promised. For my eyes have seen Your salvation, which You have prepared for all people, a light to reveal You to the nations and the glory of Your people Israel" (Luke 2:29–32).

Mary and Joseph were caught off guard by Simeon's words. They were amazed that he spoke about their son this way and wondered what his words really meant (Luke 2:33).

Simeon handed Jesus to Mary and continued to bless her family. Then, in a gentle voice, he spoke directly to Mary: "This child is destined to cause many to rise and fall in Israel, and a sword will pierce your own soul too" (Luke 2:34).

The Faithful Prophetess — Anna

In addition to Simeon, there was an elderly woman, a prophetess, who lived near the Temple, and her name was Anna. Long after her husband passed away, she spent her time worshiping, fasting, and praying to God, day and night (Luke 2:36–37).

Like Simeon, Anna also patiently waited for the day the Savior arrived at the Temple. When she saw Simeon lifting the baby and praising God, she knew in her heart that the King had come. She quickly hurried over. When she looked upon the sweet face of Jesus, joy filled her heart, and she began to worship the living God. Anna then turned around and shared the good news with everyone in the Temple courtyard, exclaiming the Messiah had finally arrived (Luke 2:38).

Mary and Joseph Find Safety in Egypt

When Herod realized he had been tricked by the Magi, he gave an order that all the boys in Bethlehem under two years old should be killed to ensure Jesus would never take his throne.

Around the same time, the Lord "appeared to Joseph in a dream and told him to take Mary and Jesus to Egypt and stay there until you hear from Me" (Matthew 2:13). So, Joseph and his family left for Egypt and stayed there until after Herod's death.

Why This Story Matters

The story of Simeon and Anna reminds us how important it is to stay consistent in our prayer life, remain present and active in our church community, and trust God's promises, even when the wait feels long. Their lives teach us that faith requires patience and that God always fulfills His word in His perfect timing, not ours.

Simeon and Anna also show us what humble confidence looks like. They weren't loud or important by the world's standards, but they were filled with God's Spirit and wisdom. Because of that, they were able to recognize Jesus for who He truly was and boldly share that truth with others.

When we follow the example of Simeon and Anna, staying faithful, prayerful, and open to God's leading, we are empowered to make a real difference. Like them, we can be a light to others and help share who God is with a world that desperately needs hope.

A Prayer to End

Dear God, help us trust You like Simeon and Anna, and to have the faith to believe that every promise You make will come true. Teach us to be patient and to wait with hope and joy, knowing that You are always at work in our lives. Strengthen our hearts so that we remain steadfast in our faith, holding firmly to Your truth no matter what challenges or blessings come our way. We give You all the praise and all the glory. Amen.

Bible References

Luke 2:22–38 — Simeon and Anna praise God when Mary and Joseph present baby Jesus at the Temple

Matthew 2:13 — Joseph and his family flee to Egypt

Conclusion

As you finish this 27-day journey from the creation of the world to the birth of Christ, my prayer for you is that you have seen the steady thread of God's love woven through every story. From the first lights that illuminated the earth to the moment Simeon and Anna praised the newborn Savior King, one truth remains constant: God's love for His people has never failed. His plan from the very beginning was to reconcile us back to Himself, and His love was so great that He sent His only Son to make that possible.

Yet this is only the beginning. The story continues in *The Easter Story: The Son*, where we follow Jesus as He grows, teaches, heals, and reveals God's purpose for each of us. There, we will walk beside Him through both joy and sorrow, witness His ultimate sacrifice on the cross, and celebrate His victory over death, where every prophecy is fulfilled and every promise of God is made complete.

Stay tuned for more!

About the Author

Gabe Rodriguez is a husband, father, and business leader whose professional career has spanned sales, marketing, and strategic planning roles for some of the nation's leading retail and consumer product companies. Known for his creativity and ability to inspire teams, Gabe has spent years bringing innovative products to market and mentoring others toward growth and purpose.

After what he describes as years of lukewarm faith, Gabe experienced a spiritual awakening that reignited his heart for Christ. This transformation inspired him to write *The Christmas Story: The Father*, a devotional created to help young adults and new believers approach the Word of God with confidence rather than fear and intimidation.

Today, Gabe writes with the same passion that fueled his professional career, but with an eternal focus: helping others build a faith that lasts for generations.

Family Scroll

Now that you have completed this book, I encourage you to record your journey with *The Christmas Story: The Father* in the Family Scroll. This is where you will document the first time, and every time after, that you have read or listened to God's story of love and redemption. Each entry is more than a note on a page. It is a marker in your walk of faith. Recording your understanding and belief in this story plants a seed of legacy, one that will grow long after you are gone. You can find more details on how to use the Family Scroll in the section at the front titled "How to Use This Book."

I was led to write this book as a real and practical way to pass my faith on to the next generation, and to offer a resource that would help others do the same. Part of the inspiration came as I read through Scripture, especially the first nine chapters of **1 Chronicles**. These chapters are filled with names, generation after generation. At first glance, they may seem like simple lists, but they tell a deeper story—who God is, how He worked through families over time, and what legacy truly means. These genealogies helped each family know where they came from, which tribe they belonged to, how God fulfilled His promises, and why faith across generations matters.

The Family Scroll was born from that biblical example. In the next pages, you will find a sample to guide you, along with a blank Family Scroll for you, your family, and even your friends to begin recording your journey of faith year after year as you read *The Christmas Story: The Father*.

My friend, the Reverend Dr. Stephen C. Lien, included a quote in his foreword that deeply resonates with me, and I want to share it again:

"I have told you before that your mother and I will probably not be able to pass on to you any kind of earthly inheritance. If we can pass on to you a passion for God, however, we will have given you something more valuable than silver, gold, or rubies and more satisfying than anything a mortal can experience."

—John Piper, *Don't Waste Your Life* (Proverbs 3:13–15)

This is the heart of the Family Scroll—to pass on a faith that endures.

Family Scroll Examples

Example 1

- Gabe is married to Michelle, and they have two sons, Benjamin and Samuel.
- It is January 2018, and Christmas 2017 has just passed.
- Gabe began reading or listening to *The Christmas Story: The Father* in December 1998 and has recorded 20 years. Using one hash mark for each year.
- Michelle began in 2006 and has recorded 12 years.
- Benjamin began in 2014 and has recorded 4 years.
- Samuel began in 2016 and has recorded 2 years.

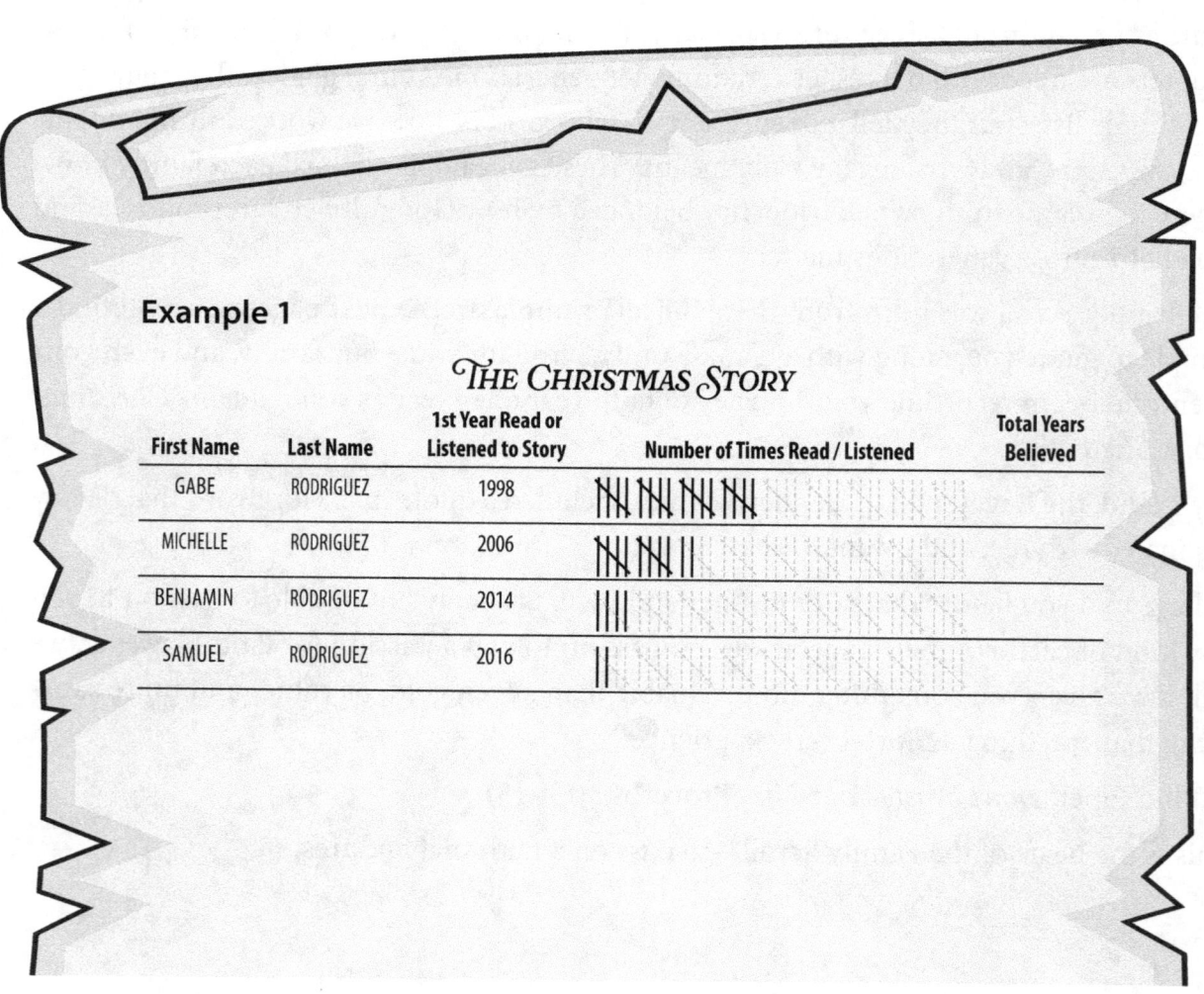

Example 1

THE CHRISTMAS STORY

First Name	Last Name	1st Year Read or Listened to Story	Number of Times Read / Listened	Total Years Believed
GABE	RODRIGUEZ	1998	卌 卌 卌 卌	
MICHELLE	RODRIGUEZ	2006	卌 卌 ||	
BENJAMIN	RODRIGUEZ	2014	||||	
SAMUEL	RODRIGUEZ	2016	||	

Example 2

- Four more Christmases have passed. It is now January 2022, and Christmas 2021 has just passed.

- Gabe and his family have added 4 additional years to their Family Scroll, recording each year they have read or listened to the story.

- Benjamin is now a senior in high school.

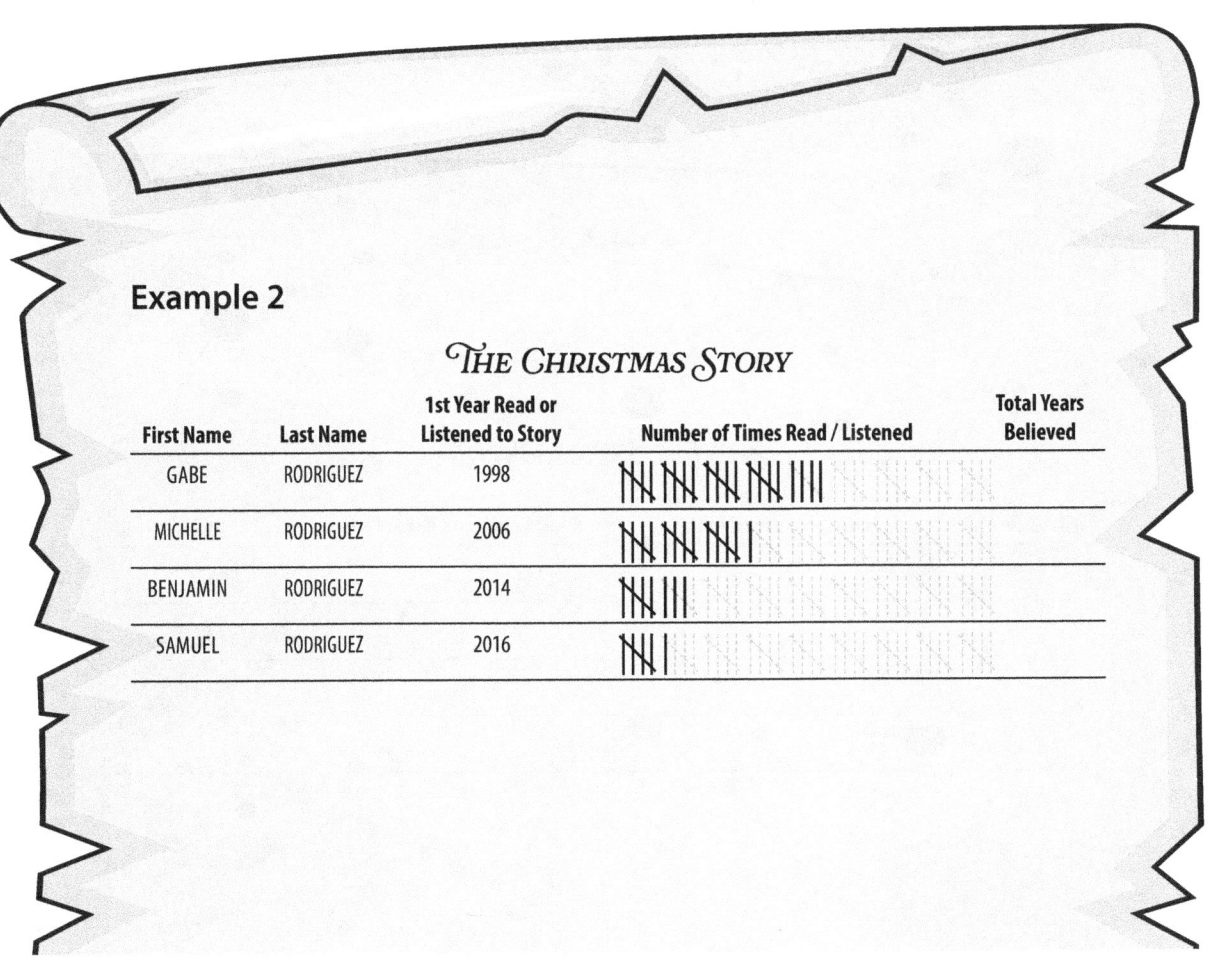

Example 2

THE CHRISTMAS STORY

First Name	Last Name	1st Year Read or Listened to Story	Number of Times Read / Listened	Total Years Believed
GABE	RODRIGUEZ	1998	|||| |||| |||| |||| ||||	
MICHELLE	RODRIGUEZ	2006	|||| |||| ||||		
BENJAMIN	RODRIGUEZ	2014	|||| |||	
SAMUEL	RODRIGUEZ	2016	||||		

Family Scroll Examples

Example 3

- Benjamin has just left for college, and Christmas 2022 is only a few months away.
- Before he leaves, his parents give him his own copy of *The Christmas Story: The Father*.
- They transfer the number of years each family member has read, listened to, and believed the story using the Total Years Believed column.
- They also transfer Benjamin's running total using hash marks for each year he has participated in the tradition.
- However, they do not total Benjamin's years in the Total Years Believed column, because he is now continuing his own family legacy.
- From this point forward, Benjamin will no longer record the years his family (Gabe, Michelle, and Samuel) continues reading *The Christmas Story: The Father*, and will now track only his own reading history.

Example 3

The Christmas Story

First Name	Last Name	1st Year Read or Listened to Story	Number of Times Read / Listened	Total Years Believed
GABE	RODRIGUEZ	1998		24
MICHELLE	RODRIGUEZ	2006		16
SAMUEL	RODRIGUEZ	2016		6
BENJAMIN	RODRIGUEZ	2014	ɪɴ̄ ɪɪɪ	

Family Scroll Examples

Example 4

- The year is now January 2033. Benjamin has been in the workforce for 8 years.

- He married Rachel in June 2029, and she began reading or listening to the story that same year.

- When Benjamin and Rachel have children who are old enough to participate (not shown here), they will record their names in the Family Scroll, along with the year they first read or listened to the story, marking each year with a hash mark.

- The cycle will continue, just as it did in Example 3. When their first child leaves home, they will purchase a new copy of *The Christmas Story: The Father* and transfer the family names and Total Years Believed into their child's Family Scroll.

- For example, if they have a son named Luke, the names transferred would include Gabe, Michelle, Samuel, Benjamin, and Rachel.

- The hope is that 40, 80, or even 120 years from now, each new reader in the same extended family will be able to see a lasting legacy of belief in the same story they now hold in their hands.

- And with that, the most important tradition continues — faith passed on from generation to generation.

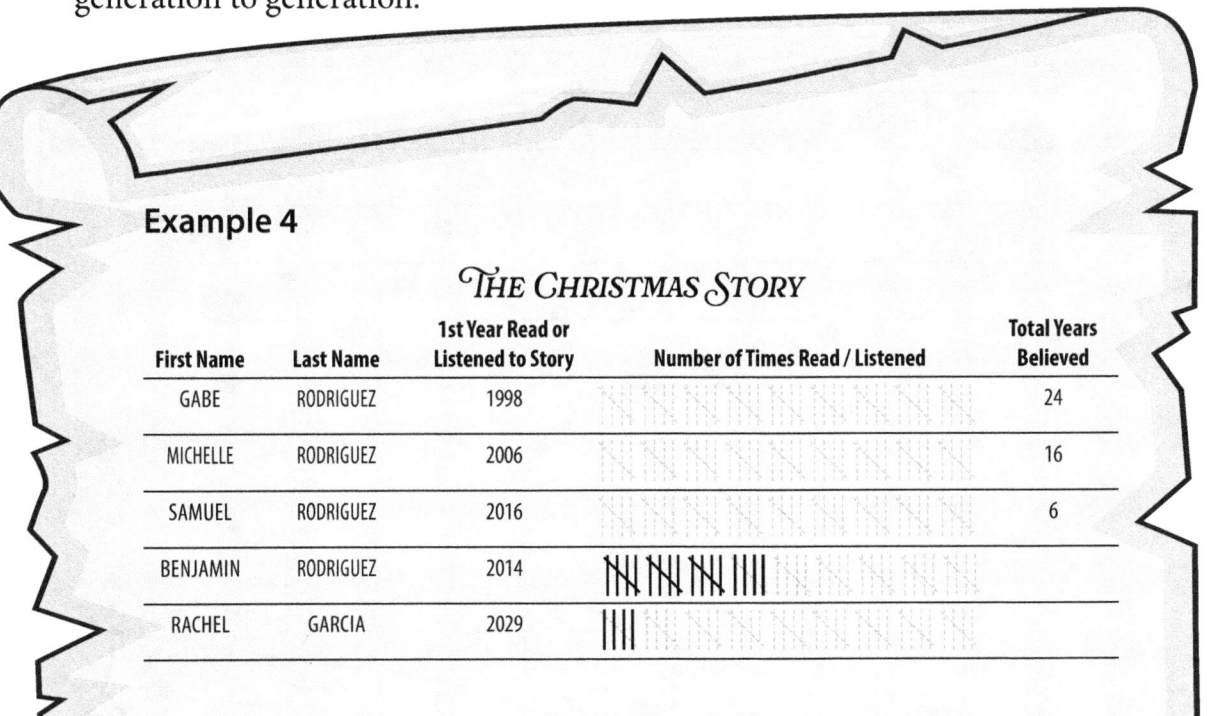

Example 4

THE CHRISTMAS STORY

First Name	Last Name	1st Year Read or Listened to Story	Number of Times Read / Listened	Total Years Believed
GABE	RODRIGUEZ	1998		24
MICHELLE	RODRIGUEZ	2006		16
SAMUEL	RODRIGUEZ	2016		6
BENJAMIN	RODRIGUEZ	2014		
RACHEL	GARCIA	2029		

FAMILY SCROLL

THE CHRISTMAS STORY

First Name	Last Name	1st Year Read or Listened to Story	Number of Times Read / Listened	Total Years Believed

FAMILY SCROLL

THE CHRISTMAS STORY

First Name	Last Name	1st Year Read or Listened to Story	Number of Times Read / Listened	Total Years Believed

FAMILY SCROLL

THE CHRISTMAS STORY

First Name	Last Name	1st Year Read or Listened to Story	Number of Times Read / Listened	Total Years Believed

FAMILY SCROLL

THE CHRISTMAS STORY

First Name	Last Name	1st Year Read or Listened to Story	Number of Times Read / Listened	Total Years Believed

Family Scroll

The Christmas Story

First Name	Last Name	1st Year Read or Listened to Story	Number of Times Read / Listened	Total Years Believed

FAMILY SCROLL

THE CHRISTMAS STORY

First Name	Last Name	1st Year Read or Listened to Story	Number of Times Read / Listened	Total Years Believed